"Homeschooling parents ha\ from-home solution, and *The 2-Second Commute* 'brings home the bacon.' The text excels with pragmatic advice and real-world examples of successful Virtual Assistants, and the exercises for strengthening the family while growing the home-based business are not to be missed."

—Rebecca Kochenderfer,
Co-founder and Senior Editor,
Homeschool.com

"Whether you're an employer or an employee, I'd bet that you had no idea what productivity gains and career opportunities your PC could offer up unless you told me you had read this book."

—Gary Moulton,
Microsoft Accessibility Technology Group
Product Manager and Co-Author,
Accessible Technology in Today's Business

"A practical, hands-on approach from someone who's 'been there.' The authors combine sound business advice with a sense of humor and don't hold back on sharing the joys, heartaches, successes, and failures of entering the realm of the self-employed VA. This book should stay open with dog-eared pages on every new VA's desk!"

—Prof. Kathy Striebel,
Lead Instructor,
Virtual Assistant Certificate Program,
MiraCosta Community College, California

"Very informative for any VA—just starting out or 'seasoned.' Military Spouses around the world should refer to this book for help with their 'virtual career' or home business."

—Carrie Lee,
a.k.a. "Sgt. Mom" (*www.SgtMoms.com*)

"Whether you work for a large organization or for yourself, in a corporate office or out of your home, you need to know how to survive in a world that's distributed, virtual, globally connected, and based largely on individual initiative and creativity. This book is a very practical, hands-on guide to the future of work, because that future is already here."

—James Ware,
Co-founder and Executive Producer,
Future of Work (*www.thefutureofwork.net*),
and former faculty member,
the Harvard Business School

"As the tidy offices of the past are relentlessly blown apart by an explosion of mobile devices, we are all increasingly working in virtual mode. This path-breaking book defines the new breed of professional assistant emerging to help out wherever we find ourselves—the Virtual Assistant."

—Prof. William E. Halal,
George Washington University,
and CEO, TechCast LLC
(*www.TechCast.org*)

2-The Second Commute

Join the Exploding Ranks of Freelance Virtual Assistants

Christine Durst
and
Michael Haaren

CAREER
PRESS

The Career Press, Inc.
Franklin Lakes, NJ

THE 2-SECOND COMMUTE
EDITED BY JODI L. BRANDON
TYPESET BY EILEEN DOW MUNSON
Cover design by Mada Design, Inc./NYC
Printed in the U.S.A. by Book-mart Press

To order this title, please call toll-free 1-800-CAREER-1 (NJ and Canada: 201-848-0310) to order using VISA or MasterCard, or for further information on books from Career Press.

The Career Press, Inc., 3 Tice Road, PO Box 687,
Franklin Lakes, NJ 07417
www.careerpress.com

Library of Congress Cataloging-in-Publication Data

Durst, Christine, 1963-
    The 2-second commute : join the exploding ranks of freelance virtual assistants / by Christine Durst and Michael Haaren.
        p. cm.
    Includes index.
    ISBN 1-56414-792-4 (paper)
    1. Virtual reality in management. 2. Administrative assistants—Computer network resources. 3. Home-based businesses—Computer network resources. 4. Business consultants—Computer network resources. I. Title: Two-second commute. II. Haaren, Michael, 1949- III. Title.

HD30.2122.D87 2005
658.3'123--dc22   2005046953

To Zachary and Laura,

for your understanding and support

as I logged long hours writing

and short hours "momming."

You are my loves, my heart,

and my greatest success stories!

—Christine Durst

To Travis and Jazz,

my beloved children,

and in the memory of

Christell Lincoln and May Lodge Ball.

—Michael Haaren

Acknowledgments

First, we would like to thank the Virtual Assistants everywhere whom we have worked with, trained, or mentored over the past 10 years. You have been one of our greatest sources of inspiration, and it has been our privilege to know you. We wish you the very best in your practices and in your personal lives as well.

In developing our Virtual Assistant training programs, we have had the great good fortune to meet some singular, gifted and dedicated people. We especially want to thank Linda Brown for having been the first person in the Pentagon to recognize the impact that Virtual Assistance might have on the career issues facing so many active-duty U.S. military spouses and their families. Linda's personal and professional commitment to these fine women and men was a constant challenge and invitation to us to try to perform at a higher level—her own. We would also like to give special thanks and recognition to Stephanie Roper-Burton; Alice "Tish" Zauner; Lt. Gen. Michael D. McGinty, USAF (Ret.), Executive

Director of the Air Force Aid Society; Linda Stephens-Jones; and Jean Marie Ward. The families and service members are indeed fortunate to have you.

Finally, our sincere thanks to the experts and Virtual Assistants whose contributions appear within. Your wisdom and insights will directly help many new and aspiring VAs as they pursue their entrepreneurial dreams.

Contents

Preface

It would have been awfully hard to predict in 1995, as Chris sat in her dingy basement office in rural Connecticut (nicknamed the "Bat Cave"), booted up her computer to help clients in Australia and the UK, and listened to the pipes thump and hiss overhead as her husband or children took a bath, that what she was doing might ever be understood even by the small town she lived in, much less the larger world.

Who could have foreseen that Virtual Assistance—this revolutionary way of working from home, and as the CEO of her own business, no less—would ultimately embrace thousands of people internationally, capture media attention from Singapore to New York, and soon find Chris talking about the "Bat Cave" and her far-flung clients to the United Nations?

And yet it happened. Community colleges in the United States and Canada now offer certificate courses in "how to be a VA," e-books are cropping up all over the Internet, and some of the largest employers in the world are encouraging their employees' "trailing spouses" to explore Virtual Assistance and virtual careers. The industry is thriving, its benefits to families, businesses, and the environment becoming manifest as telework and "homeshoring" finally take root.

But good things—strong relationships, close families, a healthy community life—take time. Rewarding, home-based careers, as does Virtual Assistance, support all three, and we are happy to join you within as you learn more about this exciting new opportunity.

Introduction

Welcome to the new business world! It's a place where a juggernaut cluster of "change agents"—the controversial but relentless trend of services outsourcing; the continually evolving Internet and other work-transmission tools; and the increasing burdens of job insecurity, suburban overcrowding, and family-hostile commutes—is birthing a whole new way of working: the *home-based virtual services career.* (Indeed, if current trends hold, business process outsourcing—of which Virtual Assistance is a part—will become the dominant form of outsourcing in 2006, says market analyst firm NelsonHall.)

It's a fact that no worker or businessperson can ignore: The global work environment is changing radically, and at a dizzying rate. Telework, downsizing, the mass outsourcing of services (if your job can be performed over a "wire," as a *Forbes* article recently pointed out, it soon will be), virtual offices and teams, metastasizing gridlock and ever-longer workweeks—combine these with millions of small businesses scarred by the last recession and determined to keep staffing and other non-core costs to a minimum, and you'll begin to see why virtual outsourcing and home-based virtual careers are among the most far-reaching developments to emerge on the American employment and family scene in quite some time.

As you'll find inside these pages, this groundbreaking movement is opening doors for people all across the working spectrum: work-at-home moms and dads, people with disabilities, home-schooling parents, family-values supporters, downsized staff and executives, "trailing" spouses, retirees, students—the list goes on and on. Whatever your own reasons for exploring the Virtual Assistant career path, we'll take you step-by-step through a proven startup and growth process that has already worked for thousands of VAs around the world.

CHAPTER 1

Why Become a Virtual Assistant?

Virtual Assistants log on at their home-based desks for a variety of reasons. Some have obligations or limitations or preferences that keep them at home (children, elderly parents, lack of transportation, physical mobility issues), others are living in areas where meaningful career opportunities are few (rural areas, developing countries), some do so out of environmental convictions, and still others find that being an "employee" simply doesn't fit.

2-Second Spotlight

"What I Love About Being a VA"

Name:	Mary Hern
Business:	Kinetic Integration, Inc.
URL:	Mary has been so busy with clients that she hasn't needed a Website.

Personal: Mary is the mother of two and an
Air Force spouse living in Norfolk,
Virginia.

Several years ago when my husband and I decided to start a family, we agreed that I would stop working and stay at home to raise the children. When my daughter turned 1, however, I began to feel like something was missing. Having worked since I was 15, I had grown used to the social interplay of a workplace, the motivation to succeed and even the need for problem-solving skills under pressure. Being at home without the demand for many of those skills, I knew something had to give.

I decided to take a more professional approach to my household. I organized closets and drawers, moved the furniture until the carpet wore thin, and developed to-do lists that brought tears to my husband's eyes. Still, I needed more. My husband asked me to put the house on a budget and find ways to cut costs. Clipping coupons and watching for sales became an obsession. I had become a "Stepford wife" and lost parts of myself that I truly missed.

Being a VA has given me the best of both worlds. I'm still at home raising my children and having a wonderful time—I still love waking up in the morning to decisions like, "Where would the tent made of blankets work best? Over the table or the couch?"—but I'm also part of something that feeds my need to interact with adults and contribute to professional society. I'm able to enjoy the details and simple triumphs of my day because when my children are tucked in bed at night, I can slip into my comfy pajamas and become the corporate woman I always dreamed of being.

As a VA, I manage projects, make decisions, and solve problems with the click of a mouse. Yet if my children need me, I'm there. If my family wants to go do something, we go. Our lives don't revolve around my work schedule, but the results of my work are tangible. I'm happier, more fulfilled and I have something to bring to the table along with a home-cooked meal. This is living.

• • • • •

Whatever the reason, once the decision is made, a successful VA enjoys some great perks: control over her life, doing only the work she loves, working only with the clients she chooses, flexibility in the work schedule for family, friends, and personal interests, and *no commute!* (In gridlocked places such as northern Virginia, where co-author Mike lives and where the commutes can reach four or more hours a day, this can be a decisive consideration.) But in our opinion, of all the reasons we've heard, the most powerful for becoming a VA is for the individual's personal and professional *freedom* and *growth.*

Freedom: The Personal Side

Why is it that when we see people with a true entrepreneurial spirit, an authentic sense of independence, there often seems to be a glow about them that no amount of fatigue or stress can overcome? The aura of some core joy seems to come shining through, no matter how heavy the responsibility that sits on their shoulders. (And some people, such as entrepreneurs with severe disabilities, are overcoming more challenges than most of us will ever know. Yet that core happiness still emerges, still prevails!)

Strange as it might sound, could it be that the air of enthusiasm and eagerness we see in them has been liberated by
the day-to-day circumstances of their lives, their own "nine-
to-five" routine?

In that single phrase is the key, we think, to the puzzle,
because entrepreneurs *have* no routine. For an entrepreneur,
the "routine" that other people submit to, and endure, and re-
enact day after day—and grow so bored with and often literally
sick of—is play, creativity, and, even better, *self-indulgence.*

Because getting up in the morning to do something you
like *is* self-indulgent. It can be likened to eating your favorite
dessert, or playing your favorite sport, or embracing those
you love. After all, this is *your* company, *your* business—a
part of yourself—and running it and shepherding it and
parenting it into the future is a tonic, a stimulant, and a provo-
cation to do better and exceed your limits—every day.

This is the deeply personal side of entrepreneurial freedom, the kind that liberates the spirit, too, and beckons the
whole self to be free. (Though beyond the scope of this book,
we believe there is most certainly a spiritual aspect to entrepreneurship, and that "good work done well" can definitely
help unfetter the spirit. Just ask any artist or craftsperson.
To do work that has no spiritual component, in our view, is
ultimately empty and can quite soon end up "emptying" the
person doing the work!)

Freedom: The Professional Side

Most of us have "worked for someone else" at some point
in our lives, and there's certainly nothing wrong with having
a job, if that's what you really want or need and if you understand what you're giving up in exchange. Jobs can be a

blessing for people who like guidance and structure, for people who prefer a fixed routine or working in group environments, and for people who like supervision. (Employment, of course, used to be a source of security, too—the comforting "pensions" of yesteryear—but that has become a rather quaint concept, these days.)

For the entrepreneurially minded, however, "employment" can be a curse, a brake, an intensely frustrating and horizon-limiting experience. *(Co-author Chris, for example, used to work as a business manager in a small office. Often, when she suggested new procedures to make the business run more effectively, she'd be met with, "It's working fine. We've been doing it this way for years!" Change is a fearful experience for those who are "employees" at heart, and the entrepreneur may often find herself stymied as she struggles to improve the organization. Nor will it help if the suggestions are being made by a woman, if the company is dominated by "old-school" men.)*

The self-employed, however—the independent-minded, the "chart-my-own-course" and "don't-fence-me-in" types—are free to be as creative and innovative as they like, free to set their own schedules and workloads, and free to say "no" when they feel like it or to say "yes" and not ask anyone's "permission" when they want to take a break, a "mental health day," or a much-needed vacation.

2-Second Spotlight

"VAs Paint Masterpieces, Too"
Name: Evelyne Matti
Business: e-Matti Virtual Business Support
            Services

URL: *www.e-matti.com.au*

Personal: Based in Sydney, Australia,
              Evelyne is married to a hotelier and
              is the proud mother of two.

My husband and my kids complain that I spend
too much time on the computer—but I love what I
do! I continually look for ways to improve my skills;
that's the fun part. Some people paint as a hobby. I
create beautiful masterpieces too, and it happens to
be part of my work! Who else can combine hobby and
work and make money at it?

• • • • •

VAs can enjoy and flourish in this freedom, too, choosing
the clients they prefer (and firing the bad ones) and deciding
where and when to work, as well as how much they want to
make while doing so. (A VA's income, where demand is a
constant, is determined directly by the quantity and quality of
his or her work and the efforts she puts into marketing.)

Moreover, a VA who has a good skill set and makes a
solid marketing effort can often earn more in her home office
than she can as an employee. (Indeed, one of the VAs we
trained recently billed $10,000 in one *month*.) In fact, accord-
ing to *The Wall Street Journal*, self-employed people who provide services are usually paid at least 20 percent to 40 percent
more per hour than employees who perform the same work.

As a self-employed person (in the United States) you'll
also be eligible for many tax benefits that employees can't
get. For example, instead of having federal and state taxes
withheld from their paychecks, self-employed people normally
pay estimated taxes directly to the IRS four times a year. This
lets you hold on to your hard-earned money longer without

having to turn it over to the taxman. Even more important, you may also be able to claim many business-related tax deductions that are available to people with home-based offices. (Be sure to check with your accountant or tax advisor to get the maximum benefits from your individual circumstances and the tax laws that apply in your location.)

Because of these tax benefits, the self-employed often pay less tax than employees who earn similar incomes.

Growth: The Personal Side

It isn't enough to be free. Freedom without growth is as wasted as a fertile garden with no plants. Having your own business and working from home—the "free" side of the equation—set the stage for your personal growth. Facing and overcoming the day-to-day challenges of running a company, however small your initial business might be, fosters tremendous personal growth in the VA. Little by little, as the independent decisions and the learning and the progress of the business accumulate, the entrepreneur begins to see herself in a totally different light—a brighter, warmer, and much more positive perspective. (And her family and friends do, too!)

For those who enjoy working with entrepreneurs, as we do, witnessing this personal growth can be one of the most gratifying parts of the "job." At the risk of sounding corny, it's a bit like seeing a butterfly coming out of its chrysalis or a young deer bounding across a meadow in the spring. In our experience there is no substitute for the sheer excitement of seeing a new entrepreneur take wing.

We mentor and train VAs from around the world and given them many of the tools and the encouragement they need to start finding their footing. But we do nothing "for" them, nothing that would substitute for their own initiative and determination and courage. (Indeed, we feel that this would be a disservice to them and would delay the day when they act "alone," and by doing so, truly grow.)

This is why it gives us such intense satisfaction to see a VA "take flight" and to receive an e-mail from someone we have never met—and perhaps never will—proclaiming in capital letters the joy she felt on discovering that she could do what she had hoped she could, achieve what she had dreamt of achieving, and telling us proudly how her self-esteem mounted as she overcame the challenges she had faced along the way.

Much has been spoken of "empowerment" over the years, be it the empowerment of minorities or women, of people with disabilities, or of other groups. And this is as it should be: Without power, we have no control over our lives, no self-determination. But one of the most empowering experiences open to anyone is to take the tiller of her own company and run it as she sees fit, to rely principally on herself for the outcome of her efforts, and to set her course, navigate her vessel through good seas and bad, and sail on to all the intriguing islands that await her—under her own willpower and strength and by her own choosing.

The Insidious Effect of "Employee Life"

Have you ever wondered about the psychological effect of working in cubes, in rooms full of people doing the same thing, following the same schedule, and all looking up at the same sterile clock? Have you ever felt the inertia, the lethargy that seeps into your mind and spirit, weighing you down as you think about the layers and layers of "decision-makers" parked over your head, all with their own fixed ideas about who you are, who you should be, what you should be doing, and how much you should be paid for it? (Actually, they're probably thinking how you're being paid *too much* for what you do and trying to figure out how to get by without you or replace you with someone cheaper.)

Have you ever found yourself putting on weight out of boredom? Snacking at the office or during a long, crawling commute, just to have a distracting sensation, a bit of pleasure, and stimulation in a dull, tedious environment?

Have you ever felt a little childish about having to ask for a "raise"? A bit sheepish and "small," as if you were a high-school student asking the teacher if you could be excused to use the rest room? (It sounds funny, but think about it!)

Ever experienced similar feelings when you had to ask some "boss" (your hands clasped deferentially in front of you) for "permission" to do something?

As you consider whether entrepreneurial life is for you (and this is not to minimize its risks), you should reflect as well on the cumulative effect of all these experiences. How have they shaped you and the way you look at yourself and your world? Do you feel, on balance, that the benefits have outweighed the costs? Are you progressing at a rate you are comfortable or happy with?

Remember that growth has many aspects: spiritual, mental, emotional, and physical. Look at all of them as you assess your situation and decide what your future will be.

Growth: The Professional Side

If the personal side of growth doesn't move you, consider the professional and financial side.

Fact 1: Market analyst firm NelsonHall predicts that business process outsourcing—of which Virtual Assistance is a part—will become the dominant form of outsourcing in 2006.

Point 1: VAs are in a high-growth industry.

Fact 2: According to Gartner, a leading IT-trends research firm, "small-business outsourcing is poised to grow appreciably over the next three to five years as chief executives strive to cut costs and raise quality."

Point 2: Because most VA clients are small businesses, VAs are in a high-growth industry both short-term and long- term.

Fact 3: According to the U.S. Bureau of Labor Statistics 2004–2005 *Occupational Outlook Handbook*, "Overall employment of secretaries and administrative assistants is expected to grow more slowly than the average for all occupations over the 2002–12 period."

This means that more than 4.1 million people—in the United States alone—who now specialize in administrative support will be competing for an ever-shrinking batch of positions in the larger companies.

Point 3: Traditional administrative-related opportunities are shrinking.

Fact 4: Speaking again of the United States, the Small Business Administration reports that there are now 23.7 million small businesses (defined as having less than 500 employees) and that these generate 60–80 percent of new jobs every year. Millions of these businesses are home-based, and their revenues (as well as their numbers) are growing. But despite their growth, home-based business owners do not normally want employees present in their homes. Outsourcing is the answer, which is one reason why small-business outsourcing generally is predicted to grow appreciably over the next three to five years. (We ourselves expect strong micro-business outsourcing growth as broadband Internet achieves full distribution and continues to evolve, and as full-quality videoconferencing comes into play.)

Point 4: Small businesses generally and home-based businesses in particular are the primary source of clients for VAs. In other words, a sizeable segment of the VA client pool is growing in number, revenues, and outsourcing flow.

Fact 5: According to the International Telework Association and Council, there are 24.1 million employed teleworkers and 16.5 million self-employed teleworkers in the United States today. For both groups, this increasingly popular arrangement allows them the freedom to help balance their career and home life. For the HR manager, however, the trend poses new problems, because research shows that the majority of teleworkers work mostly during non-business hours (including holidays) and hence often need a more flexible administrative support system than "HQ" can provide. And for the self-employed teleworker, who is usually psychologically or financially disinclined to bring an employee into his or her home, there may be no administrative support available at all.

Point 5: HR managers who are grappling with how to provide top-notch support to their offsite workers now have—and are using—the VA option. Indeed, a small group of VAs, each working "by the hour," can undergird a number of teleworkers cost-effectively across locations and time zones both, and—being "offsite" themselves—will often understand the offsite workers' needs much better than the assistant back at the office. And the same solution—larger or smaller as the case requires—fits the self-employed teleworker as well.

Given these trends, it seems fairly certain there will be a strong demand for virtual support services for many years to come.

CHAPTER 2

Exploring Virtual Assistance

When co-author Chris founded the Virtual Assistance industry back in 1995, people in her neck of the woods had a hard time "getting their minds around" what she was up to. Friends and family would politely inquire, "So, what exactly is it you're doing now?" Delighted to share her excitement, she would pitch into a monologue about the Internet, and the trend toward small business startups, and corporate downsizing, and the coming of broadband, and file transfers, and how her Website was developing. But much to her chagrin, their eyes soon glazed over and blank expressions overtook their faces. (Eventually, she decided to keep it simple by replying, "I use the Internet to help businesspeople with their administrative tasks from my office instead of theirs.")

Usually, at this point listeners would feel that they had done their duty, and someone would give her a pat on the arm and say, "That's nice, dear. Would you like another piece of pie?"

Since then, the industry has grown so rapidly that the challenge is no longer how to explain "what Virtual Assistants do," but to sort through the diverse interpretations of Virtual Assistance to clarify the core concept.

Virtual Assistance Defined

Reducing the idea to its basic elements—two words: *virtual* and *assistance*—can simplify things straight away. *Virtual* describes something that can be done or seen using a computer, and therefore without going anywhere or talking to anyone (*Cambridge Advanced Learner's Dictionary*), and *assistance* is the act of assisting or the help supplied (*Merriam-Webster Dictionary*). The industry has also earned a full-blown definition in Microsoft's Encarta World English Dictionary (*encarta.msn.com*). The Encarta definition is:

> *vir·tu·al as·sis·tant (plural vir·tu·al as·sis·tants) noun, long-distance assistant: somebody who uses computer and phone connections to work from a distance as a personal assistant to somebody else, instead of working in the same office or building.*

Nearly every VA has a "What is a Virtual Assistant?" link on his or her Website, but are they all using the same definition? Hardly! Try typing the phrase "what is a virtual assistant" (with the quotes) into Google (one of our favorite search engines), and you'll get more than 3,000 returns. Many of the sites listed in those returns will be using a "canned" definition of Virtual Assistance—one that has been borrowed from another source. For example, there are literally hundreds of VAs who still use the copy we created when we launched Staffcentrix in 1999:

Like the majority of their clients, Virtual Assistants are entrepreneurs—highly skilled in their profession and able to have a powerful impact on the productivity of those they work with. Traditionally, they have been known by many names: secretaries, administrative assistants, executive assistants or bookkeepers. But in an age where technology has made the world a much smaller place, and where more professionals are working from their homes or in satellite offices, the former assistant has become virtual—and thanks to the Internet, global.

(Even after all these years, we feel this statement provides a clear and concise idea of what VAs do, though it would be nice to see a few more permissions statements on all those pages where it's used. *Hint, hint!*)

The International Virtual Assistants Association (IVAA; *www.ivaa.org*), the industry's nonprofit parent organization, also offers a concise definition:

A Virtual Assistant (VA) is an independent entrepreneur providing administrative, creative and/or technical services. Utilizing advanced technological modes of communication and data delivery, a professional VA assists clients in his/her area of expertise from his/her own office on a contractual basis.

Still other organizations, such as AssistU (*www.assistu.com*), prefer to use what might be considered more of a "boutique" definition of Virtual Assistance. Their position is that a true VA offers *only* administrative and personal support, and *only* to clients who agree to a long-term, "committed" relationship. Although we ourselves tend to view Virtual Assistance in broader terms, AssistU's positioning shows the variety of interpretations that have evolved since the industry's beginnings.

When a VA is launching his or her business, there are so many things to think about that, when it comes time to draft original text for a Website or other marketing materials, the creative juices may just seem to dry up. When this happens, a canned description can be a good starting point. Otherwise, however, we suggest that VAs remain flexible and let their operational definition of Virtual Assistance stay supple and evolve as the business evolves. Moreover, your definition, whether dynamic or final, will depend largely on who you are, what services you're offering, and the types of clients you prefer to work with.

Regardless of their uniqueness, as you review the definitions and positioning developed by other VAs, you'll find common themes, phrases, and concepts. For example:

- ✦ "Home-based entrepreneurs."
- ✦ "Small-business owners, like their clients."
- ✦ "Virtual administrative or executive assistants."
- ✦ "Highly-trained professionals."
- ✦ "Long-term, collaborative partners."
- ✦ "Use the telephone, e-mail, fax, and the Internet to communicate with their clients."

Clients will vary in their location and business type, and skills and services will vary from VA to VA, but the core concept remains the same: Virtual Assistance is "professional help from afar."

A Word on Plagiarism

While we're discussing the possibility of using "canned" text on a Website, it seems to be an appropriate time to remember that "posting" and "plagiarizing" can often go hand in hand. (We're not attorneys, and this isn't legal advice, but we'd be remiss if we didn't at least raise the issue to help you avoid coming to grief.) The Internet has made it possible for almost anyone to publish their original works at will for unlimited numbers to see, providing greater opportunity for the honest and dishonest alike. If you find text that you'd like to include on your Website or other materials, be sure to obtain written permission before using it. Even if you don't see a copyright or trademark notice near the text, the protection is broad, and it's still best to assume that the law applies. (The same caveat applies to graphics, photos, and any other original works.)

In your request, tell the person exactly what you'd like to use and how you'd like to use it. Include information about your business so the copyright holder can make an informed decision. Remember: Copyright owners may have any one of a number of reasons to decline permission—ranging from perceived competition to fears of losing control of their material—so if the answer is no, accept it graciously and move on. If the answer is yes, be sure to include a permissions statement on every page that includes the material you're using. (As an example, we grant permission for the online use of certain text we've authored, but only when the following statement appears near the material: "Portions of the content herein © 2005, by Staffcentrix, LLC. Used with permission."

A final word: Don't believe the common fallacy that "tweaking" a few words here and there will make it your own work. That's like pushing bits of chocolate into store-bought sugar cookies and claiming you made chocolate chip cookies from scratch.

VA Demographics and Work Practices: The "Who," "How," and "What" of the Industry

As an industry that's still in its youth, Virtual Assistance presents a challenge for those taking polls and surveys. The problem is the absence of a comprehensive international VA registry, or even in many cases country-specific registries. (There are some, but not many, and partly because Virtual Assistants are by definition independent individuals. With the entrepreneur's "go my own way" streak, directories and rosters often capture only a portion of their true numbers.) Complicating matters, many VA sites are not search engine–optimized, even some of the most successful VAs do not have Websites, and many new VAs with one or two clients put off building a Web presence indefinitely. For researchers, attempting to locate and contact every active VA is pragmatically impossible.

However, our company, Staffcentrix, has been a leader in the Virtual Assistant industry since its founding in 1999, training, teaching, or mentoring more than 3,800 VAs internationally, and we have compiled a great deal of data on the field through periodic surveys and polls, as well as an extensive archive of communications. Most recently, Staffcentrix surveyed more than 2,000 Virtual Assistants from 35 countries on a wide range of issues. Here are some of the results:

✦ The VA population is by far more female than male (98%).

✦ A variety of "life situations" and other reasons, alone or in combination, motivate individuals to launch a VA business:

◆ Work-at-home parent	50%
◆ "Displaced homemaker"	04%
◆ "Trailing spouse"	19%
◆ Home-caring for sick or elderly family member	08%
◆ Student	06%
◆ Retiree	02%
◆ Person with a disability	06%
◆ Downsized executive/administrative professional	19%
◆ Living in an area of low employment (that is, rural)	14%
◆ Temporary employee seeking self-employment	15%

✦ The majority (45%) of VAs prefer to work part-time in their businesses so they can balance family and personal commitments.

✦ About 30% of VAs are also working outside the home but plan to discontinue doing so as soon as their businesses are generating enough income.

✦ VAs are offering a steadily growing range of services. Listed on the following pages are some of the more popular specialties:

Academic Writing

Accounting Services

Audiovisual Production

Business Coaching

Business Plan Writing

Business Writing

Calendaring/Appt. Scheduling

Collection Services

Competitive Research

Concierge Services

Database Management

Desktop Publishing

Document OCR/Scanning

Editing/Proofreading

E-mail Screening

Entertainment Industry Support

Event Planning

File Conversion

Fundraising

General Transcription

Government Procurement Expertise

Grant Proposals

Graphic Design/Scanning

Growth Advisory Services

HR Expertise

Insurance Broker Support

Internet Research

Interpreting

Import-Export Support

Intranet Development/ Mgmt.

Legal Secretary

Legal Transcription

Litigation Support

Live Phone Answering

Mailing Services

Marketing/Advertising

Market Research

Medical Transcription

Multimedia Presentation

Nonprofit Support Services

Office Management

Paralegal Services

Payroll Services

Phone-in Transcription

Photography

Private Investigation Support

Programming

Public Relations

Real Estate Support	Technical Writing/Editing
Reminder Services	Translating Services
Resume Writing	Voice Services
Spreadsheets	Voicemail for Clients
Statements/Billing	Website Design
Systems Management	Word Processing

•••••

It's worth noting that most of the services included in the previous list can embrace a variety of activities or sub-specializations. For example, a VA who offers "Real Estate Support" may provide a range of services, including coordinating direct mail campaigns, paying bills, preparing a daily schedule, confirming appointments, preparing relocation packages, uploading new listings to the client's Website, and so forth. Likewise, a VA offering "Import-Export Support" might provide everything from basic administrative support to competitive research to a low-cost office presence for an offshore firm.

What Are VAs Charging for Their Services?

Virtual Assistants generally charge $25–35 per hour for general administrative support services. (Clients pay more, of course, for specialized or higher-echelon services.) At first glance these rates may appear steep, but statistics show that employees actually cost two to two-and-a-half times their hourly rate of pay when employers factor in the cost of recruitment, base salary, employment taxes, mandatory insurance, benefits, physical space, and equipment. In other words, an employee being paid $12 an hour is actually costing the employer between $25 and $30 per hour. If you add to this various "employee side effects" that you can't put a price tag on—personality conflicts; socializing while on the clock; legal exposure for sexual harassment, discrimination, OSHA and other employee-related liabilities; frequent interruptions to workflow and lower productivity generally—you'll see that VAs truly are an economical solution for many businesses.

Each year, Staffcentrix surveys thousands of Virtual Assistants for its "Work Practices & Fee Survey." Here is a sampling of the average rates reported for various services in our most recent survey (2004/2005).

Service	Hourly Fee (U.S. Dollars)
Accounting Services	34
Business Coaching	50
Concierge Services	33
Database Management	39
Editing/Proofreading	33
General Transcription	30
Graphic Scanning	28
Internet Research	33
Litigation Support	35
Mailing Services	25
Multimedia Presentations	47
Spreadsheets	32
Translating Services	39
Word Processing	28

• • • • •

Again, these fees are averages and will also vary according to currency exchange rates and other influences. Later in the book we'll discuss some of the factors you'll want to take into account as you determine your own fee schedule.

Why Businesses Are Hiring Virtual Assistants: Changing Workplace, Changing Needs

Virtual Assistance, which in 1995 seemed like something out of a science fiction novel, has become so mainstream (even that most mainstream of magazines, *Time*, recently ran an article on the industry titled "At Your Service") that the question "What is a VA?" is steadily being replaced with "Who is your VA?"

If we had to explain the growing popularity of VAs, we'd point to three key factors:

1. The increasing costs (and headaches) of having employees.
2. The broad dispersion of talent that is willing and able to work.
3. The global growth of the Internet, enabling businesses to find and use the best candidates for non-core tasks regardless of location.

It's a fact no businessperson can ignore: The workplace and the workforce are changing rapidly, much of it through outsourcing, which has become such an established trend that the word scarcely draws any attention anymore (unless your job is the one that got scrapped). Consider just some of the more obvious benefits that businesspeople gain by outsourcing to VAs:

Diverse Expertise Across Global Markets

VAs bring a wide array of skills and experience to the business table and represent an on-the-ground resource in a variety of markets both domestic and foreign. From data entry to customer service support to on-site market research, there is a VA for almost every non-core task. (Well, they don't do windows, just Windows.)

Time Savings

Because businesses can afford to be pickier when they choose a VA than when they're drawing from the local labor base (an international Net-connected talent pool of thousands of people makes this possible), they don't need to spend nearly as much time—dead, non-profit time—training and prepping and supervising the "newbie," particularly where a specialty is concerned. Experienced VAs "ramp up" quickly and often have very similar businesses among their active clients. Further, as an independent offsite contractor, the VA avoids the distractions and "slack time" typical of the conventional work environment (teleworkers are well-known for their higher productivity) and is free to concentrate on the matter at hand.

Ulcer-Free Hiring and Firing, and Improved Project Management

When hiring a VA, the client can not only be more selective, but can "switch horses" much more easily if the new hire doesn't work out. How so? As any lawyer will likely tell you, firing an independent contractor is nothing like firing an employee (a gut-wrenching process in the best of circumstances), and changing from one independent contractor to another is infinitely simpler and faster than "switching" employees. ("Here, let's just fire Jane and hire John and we'll be back on track tonight!") Moreover, projects often have a habit of "morphing" as they develop, making it problematic when the employee with skill set A is suddenly asked to execute using skill set Q. Adding a VA "Q" specialist to handle or finish the job can often be much easier than adjusting the employee mix— or suddenly asking Mr. A to train to become Mr. Q, too.

Keeps On-Site Staff Focused!

Partnering with VAs frees up on-site staff to focus on their own core competencies (and preferred work), making the entire organization more efficient and effective.

Cost Control

Outflow is easier to manage with VAs, because costs flow clearly and directly from the project. (Contrast this with the usual expense picture of projects and assignments, where employee training, expense accounts, insurance, taxes, benefits, and so on tend to mix in a wasteful puzzle.)

Commitment and Aligned Interests

The VA has a vested interest in helping her clients succeed, because his or her own business depends on it. (Employees rarely have as much at risk as the entrepreneur, and they never have the same mindset.)

Limited Obligations and Expenses

Because the VA is a contractor, the client avoids having to deal with time-consuming and expensive tax, legal and insurance issues—even when not "hiring and firing."

The chart on pages 40–41 shows how significant the tax, legal, and insurance advantages of hiring a VA can be, along with other critical "bottom line" differences between employees and VAs.

VAs vs. Employees		
Obligation / Benefit	**Employee**	**VA**
Hirer pays only for "Time on Task" or by project.		X
Can be a sounding board when needed.		X
Helps hirer stay on track and on schedule.		X
Handles seasonal or periodic projects.		X
No need to buy additional hardware (computer, fax, PDAs, etc.).		X
No computer training needed.		X
Convenient when on-site staff gets overloaded.		X
No time wasted on breaks or personal issues.		X
Works on an "as-needed" basis.		X
No extra office space required; no extra rent or loss of privacy for the home-based hirer.		X
No need to buy extra desk, chair, phone, or supplies.		X
Hirer must pay employer social security taxes.	X	
Hirer must collect and pay FICA taxes.	X	
Hirer must pay worker's compensation insurance.	X	

VAs vs. Employees (continued)		
Obligation / Benefit	**Employee**	**VA**
Hirer must pay federal and state unemployment taxes.	X	
Hirer must comply with OSHA.	X	
Hirer must comply with the Federal Fair Labor Standards Act (FFLSA), including minimum wage and overtime payment.	X	
Hirer must comply with Employee Retirement Income Security Act (ERISA).	X	
Hirer may have to pay medical benefits, dental, vision, etc.	X	
Hirer may have to pay vacation time, sick time and holiday time.	X	
Hirer may have to fund other employee benefits such as 401K, other retirement plans, etc.	X	
Hirer must pay someone to administer the above benefits.	X	
Hirer has legal exposure that includes working hours, sexual harassment, discrimination, vacation time, sick time, leaves of absence, holidays, benefits, performance reviews, grievances, terminations, substance abuse, obligatory training, etc.	X	
In the event of layoffs, hirer's unemployment rate may increase for years to come.	X	

3 Scenarios to Illustrate the Point

To give you a better idea why VAs are quickly becoming so popular internationally, we've outlined three detailed scenarios where the VA plays a pivotal and cost-effective role.

Scenario 1: The VA and the SOHO (Small Office/Home Office)

As the U.S. Small Business Administration (SBA) and other authorities tell us, increasing numbers of entrepreneurs are abandoning the problems and politics of traditional corporate life to launch their own home-based businesses. Armed with a great idea and a healthy measure of backbone, they dive in with gusto, marketing their service or product online and off. These efforts make their business grow, but success also means mounting stacks of paper, more phone traffic, correspondence, post-sale clean-up, time paying bills, tracking expenses, and communications and appointments—in short, a torrent of non-essential chores. At this point, they've succeeded in reaching what we call the *entrepreneurial impasse*: The SOHO businessperson has become his own (bogged-down) administrative staff, in addition to the key employee!

Previously, the SOHO would have had limited choices: hire an expensive (and sometimes unmotivated) "temp" for a transient solution; take on expense and responsibility with a permanent employee; or, worst of all, turn away the work. But Virtual Assistance offers a new and better option. An independent businessperson in her own right, the VA can handle those non-core tasks cost-effectively from a distance—outside that cramped office—so the SOHO can focus on efforts that drive the bottom line.

Scenario 2: The VA and the Downsizing and "Flat-Sizing" Company

Many larger businesses in the United States and other developed countries are either downsizing or flat sizing (foregoing new hires) to do battle with foreign competitors or to contend with domestic competitors who—as they are—are outsourcing at home or offshore. As these businesses reconfigure their workflows or executive and staff structures and the changes ripple through the organization, they often run into problems dealing with their administrative and related needs. For each, VAs offer a ready solution.

Problem 1: In both the downsizing and flat-sizing company, the administrative personnel—demoralized in the first case from firings, and in the second from the company's reluctance to add employees—are running hard to keep pace with the workflow. This exacerbates the morale problem and costs overtime and comp time.

VA Solution: When workflow outstrips the staff or swells during a crisis or influx of new business, VAs can step in as short-term or long-term help. When work ebbs, the company has no termination headaches, no employee downtime, and no unemployment issues. (And the same VAs—who now know the client's needs and its niche and internal workings as well—are standing by to help meet the next crunch at a moment's notice.)

Problem 2: The downsized company's workflow has thinned to the point that the administrative staff is busy only sporadically and is getting paid for "shuffling papers."

VA Solution: When the workflow becomes too slow to justify current staff strength, and further layoffs and adjustments have to be made, VAs can step in to help as needed during and after the transition. If a "skeleton staff" is kept, VAs can stand by to handle overflow whenever it occurs, enabling the company to "expand and contract" as necessary and be more responsive to changes in its niche. (Indeed, some smaller enterprises discover that almost all support tasks can be handled virtually, leaving the core team to concentrate on what's really important: growing the business.)

• • • • •

Scenario 3: The VA as an Offshore Office

Although most VA-client relationships are within the same country, one of the many benefits VAs offer is the chance for the smaller business to have an offshore presence without the expense of employees or stand-alone offices. For example, a small-business owner in Buenos Aires desiring a presence in the United States only has to hire a U.S.–based VA to instantly acquire a U.S. mailing address, phone and fax number, e-mail address, courier and other services, and local or regional on-the-ground liaison and expertise.

By the same token, an American, European, or Asian businessperson seeking an Argentine presence need only follow a similar route through an Argentine VA.

2-Second Spotlight

Benefits to Clients of Having a Foreign-Based VA
Name: Lyn Prowse-Bishop, MVA, ASO
Business: Executive Stress Office Support
                  (eSOS)

URL: *www.execstress.com*

Personal: Based in Brisbane, Australia, with
            clients in the United States, the
            UK, and Australia, Lyn provides
            offshore and domestic support to
            independent professionals, con-
            sultants, and small and medium-
            sized businesses.

Working with a VA overseas has many advantages,
not the least of which is that the client effectively has
a 24-hour business. Work can be completed while the
client sleeps, so for functional purposes, their "office"
never closes. It is also highly efficient—the client can
draft a document and have it turned around overnight.

In addition, a client might require an overseas
presence, overseas address, and foreign "accent" if
they are planning to grow their business internationally or need a VA to communicate or liaise with the
client's existing customers, suppliers, or partners located in the VA's country. Foreign-based VAs can also
perform cost-effective local research, a task that might
prove cost-prohibitive if clients attempted to do this
for themselves.

Then there are the financial benefits. Many VAs
charge only in their home currency, and if the exchange
rate is favorable to clients, they can receive quality
services for a fraction of the price that an in-country
VA would charge.

• • • • •

The VA Industry Abroad

Although the Virtual Assistant industry was born in the
United States, it has quickly gained members and supporters

abroad, with VAs now hailing from more than 35 countries around the globe. While writing this book we spoke with several leading "offshore" VAs to get a snapshot of what's happening beyond our home turf, and we'll share their perspectives here.

Canada

We asked pioneering Canadian VA Michelle Jamison, president of MJVA (*www.mjva.ca*), founding member of the Canadian VA Network, and author of *The Virtual Assistant's Guide to Marketing*, to give us her viewpoint on the VA industry in Canada.

"It's a very exciting time for Canadian VAs," Michelle replied. "Canadians are recognizing the value of working at home and of hiring independent contractors such as Virtual Assistants to help. In the past three years in particular, VAs have been receiving more media attention than ever, and we've seen an increase in resources and support networks for the newer VA."

Michelle also noted that more than half of the self-employed in Canada are operating home-based businesses, which, as in the United States, spells opportunity for Virtual Assistants. "These are individuals who don't have the space to hire on-site assistance and need relief from the day-to-day administrative headaches of running a business. As their numbers continue to grow, so will the need for skilled VAs."

Again, as in the United States, only a small fraction of Canada's home-based businesspeople, estimated to number 500,000, currently works with a VA, so this is very much a "ground-floor opportunity."

In addition to increased media coverage, resources, and networks, Michelle points to other growth signs in the VA arena. "We're also seeing an increase in Virtual Assistant training programs. In 2003, Red Deer College, in Red Deer, Alberta, became the first accredited educational institute in Canada to recognize Virtual Assistance as a profession and is offering an extensive VA training program." Michelle feels this is a harbinger of good things to come. "With the success of the Red Deer College program, more and more educational institutes will begin to offer VA training. This in itself will only add to the viability and credibility of the VA industry in Canada."

United Kingdom

For insights on Britain, we checked in with leading UK VA Bridget Postlethwaite, co-founder of the International Association of Virtual Assistants (*www.iava.org.uk*) and managing director of IAVA Ltd. (Bridget actually resides in the Channel Islands off the coast of France, which gives her a unique perspective on things British.)

Bridget prefaced her remarks by pointing out that some British employers have been slow to grasp the benefits of working with Virtual Assistants, in part because they've lacked awareness of the availability of qualified VAs to meet their needs. However, she sees this changing as more British PAs (Personal Assistants) opt to become VAs and, on the client side, as self-employment and entrepreneurship grow.

"In recent years," Bridget says, "the sharp decline in the quality of public transport in the UK—particularly buses and trains in the more outlying areas—has led PAs who used to travel some distance to work to look at alternative options, such as Virtual Assistance. With the publicity that's been given to virtual working and the IAVA over the last four years, the opportunities to become a VA and to find clients have offered an ideal springboard for this group of people."

On the hiring side, Bridget sees a robust future. "The general trend in the UK appears to be much more towards 'self-employment' and 'entrepreneurial' work, which inevitably will benefit VAs as more and more of their potential clients cease to operate from traditional offices, or indeed to work the standard nine-to-five. Increasingly, businesspeople are valuing the flexibility of working hard when they are working, and taking time with families and to pursue outside interests when the work is done."

Though it's obvious from her observations that UK VAs can't let up on their marketing, "the future in the UK," Bridget concludes, "is quite positive."

Ireland

The VA industry is new to Ireland, and to get the download we spoke with Belfast-based VA Margaret McKillen. As we go to press, Margaret, who runs Just Write Secretarial Services (*www.jw-ss.com*), has recently taken the visionary step of founding the Association of Virtual Assistants of Ireland (*www.avaireland.com*), resulting in growing coverage in the local and national media.

"Although the VA industry is in its infancy here, Ireland, with the development of its 'Celtic Tiger' economy, is very progressive in adopting modern technology. This 'boom' economy has created a labor shortage in specialist disciplines within the administration area. It has also given administration professionals the confidence to become self-employed within the VA market."

Margaret sees the VA industry's youth in Ireland as a distinct advantage, because the benefits that businesses derive from working with VAs have a proven track record elsewhere, and this can easily be referenced online. "Ireland can learn a lot from the U.S. and the UK regarding the VA industry," she says. "An employer has only to look at the success rate the VA has had abroad to know that it's definitely the way forward regarding office administration."

• • • • •

So ends our introduction to the Virtual Assistance industry. At this point, you should have a basic sense of what the industry is all about and how you might fit into it. Now it's time to see if you're ready to make the move into self-employment generally and Virtual Assisting specifically.

CHAPTER 3

Reality Checks and Self-Assessments

Starting a home-based business can quickly touch almost every part of your life (and where families are involved, theirs as well) and should never be undertaken lightly. Money, health, expectations, dreams—and love itself—can all be put at risk. Preparation is everything.

In this chapter, we'll take a look at some of the issues that should be weighed carefully before you and yours go into business. (Here it might be a good idea to grab a pen and paper so you can write down your thoughts as we ask you some core pre-trip questions.)

Your Motives

Failing to have a good grasp of your motives for starting a business can quickly lead you to disappointment and frustration, if not the failure of your entire venture. So we always advise prospective Virtual Assistants to take a careful and objective look at what's really driving their interest, *before* they leap.

We've worked with thousands of VAs over the years, and shortly we'll get into the more typical reasons they cite for choosing the VA path. But before we do, let's spend a moment on some of the other motivations, ones that don't fit as well into the VA niche.

We're talking about unrealistic expectations, and folks who don't have a good grip on how VAing works. These individuals (or sometimes their spouses or companions, who for better or worse are participating heavily in the decision-making) hope to get rich quick, or imagine having lots of "spare time," or want to impress their friends or relatives with a high-cost lifestyle. There's nothing wrong with strong motivation—people need it for any worthwhile entrepreneurial endeavor—but expecting to get rich quickly (if at all) as a VA, or looking for leisure time, or leasing the "Beemer" at the first opportunity is not the way to go. If you "expect" to get rich as a VA you probably won't, and if you want to relax, you'd be better off spending the money on a vacation from your present job or situation. (Entrepreneurs rarely relax, by the way, and successful ones more rarely still!) As for leasing that expensive car, well, you'll be far less tempted when you realize who's got to pay for it—you, because "you" and your business are one and the same.

2-Second Spotlight

"I've Found Work-Life Balance"
Name: Evy Williams
Business: Brochures By Design.com
URL: *www.BrochuresByDesign.com*

Personal: Evy Williams, an active-duty military spouse, is stationed in Augusta, GA, with her husband and their three children. She specializes in professional writing services and desktop publishing. She has a Master's degree and is currently the Managing Editor of IVAACast, the official publication of the International Virtual Assistants Association.

Being a VA, I've found the perfect work-life balance for myself. I'm available to my family when they need me, yet I can still take time to fulfill my career goals.

I didn't want my children to grow up and feel I hadn't made myself available to them. I wanted to be able to share each and every day with them while I was able. Someday, they'll be grown and gone, but we will have positive memories of their childhoods. Having a home-based business allows me the freedom to work around their schedules. For this, I am grateful: I can help provide for my family as well as be there for them.

• • • • •

When we ask trainees or mentees why they want to become VAs, they typically point to one or more of the following:

★ I want a new challenge in my life.

★ I want to be home with my children, but we need a second income.

★ I was under-appreciated in past positions, or am in my current job.

★ I want more flexibility in my schedule.

✯ I want a career that blends and balances with the needs of my family.

✯ I have a disability that makes it difficult for me to work outside my home or in a traditional work environment.

✯ I am under-employed.

✯ I am unemployed.

✯ I live in a location that has limited job opportunities in my field.

✯ I live in a rural location where there are few jobs of any kind.

✯ I work in an environment where my ideas are not allowed to surface and others are given credit for my accomplishments.

✯ I am a "trailing spouse," and the constant job changes have been detrimental to my career.

✯ I've been downsized out of a job.

✯ My commute leaves me too little personal or family life.

✯ I homeschool my children, and need to be home with/for them.

✯ With the cost of gas, a work wardrobe, dry cleaning, lunches, tolls, auto maintenance, and childcare, I was making less than minimum wage in my job.

✯ I want to provide a second income for my family.

✯ I retired and discovered that I want to keep working.

Any of these reasons may be sound and will be even more sound to the degree the speaker has evaluated her or his circumstances, personality, and skill sets.

Now take a few minutes to write down your own reasons for wanting to launch your business. Keep in mind that it's all right to be "selfish" in your motives: sometimes our wants can motivate us much more powerfully than our needs.

Financial Considerations

Your ability to support yourself and others who may depend on you will probably be one of your primary concerns as you move forward—which is why starting a business may be one of the most frightening things you'll ever do. True, every day people of all persuasions abandon the security of company-funded insurance and retirement plans, salaries, and vacations for the great adventure of launching their own "gig." *But how much financial risk are you yourself willing to take?* It's a question every entrepreneur must ask.

Taking an honest look at your finances is a critical first step. Do you have the cash reserves to pay your present and projected bills until your business turns a profit? Whether or not you currently have a job, you must have an adequate "nest egg" before you start, something to carry you through the initial three to six months—more if you're currently working full-time—that you'll need to get up and running and see your marketing efforts begin to bear fruit. Take stock of your savings and, if you find they're a bit short, try juggling the budget so you can direct more money into your cushion. Even when starting a business in an industry that's booming, you'll initially have more bills than income, so be prepared to see steady red ink before black.

In our Virtual Assistant training classes, we try to avoid repeating information or advice unnecessarily. But as any graduate will confirm, we ignore the rule when it comes to telling new VAs, "If you have a job now, don't leave it!"

Easing into your VA practice a few hours a day and/or on weekends is one of the safest and least stressful ways to make the change, and many new VAs take this route, building their practice one after-hours brick at a time. However, it still requires planning. On the VA side, make sure your clients understand your limited availability from the start (Beware of those clients who don't!) and be sure to factor in the impact that the transitional arrangement will have on the significant others in your life (spouses or companions, kids, and so forth). You're certain to be working longer hours overall as you establish your VA practice, and you won't be as available emotionally or physically to your family or friends as you were before the change.

On the job side, be sure not to take on extra responsibilities that will squelch or undo your part-time VA efforts or disappoint your boss or any current VA clients. A bad reference from your current employer—who is a potential future client, keep in mind—or bad word of mouth from a present VA client is the last thing you want, so juggle prudently and adroitly!

Next, work on figuring out how much income you'll need to meet your existing financial obligations, cover new business expenses, and have some extra to help you achieve some of your larger goals. Be a bit liberal when calculating this figure—it's far better to discover you have more money than you planned on than to find yourself short.

Once you've come up with an "income needed" amount, determine how many hours you'll have to bill each week to reach that goal. For example, if you need $500 a week in income, and you plan on billing $25 an hour for your services, you'll have to generate 20 billable hours each week ($25 × 20 = $500).

If after launching your business you discover that expenses exceed your income, you'll have to rebalance the equation. This may mean increasing your billable hours, cutting your expenses, pursuing additional clients, and/or increasing your rates. Ask yourself if you and your family will be willing to adapt to these changes if circumstances demand it. Reduced expenses means tighter budgets. More working hours means less family time. Finding new clients also takes time, and raising your rates may make sales tougher and more stressful. Again, be prepared.

This is probably a good time to remind you that you won't be paid for all the hours you work—far from it. Self-employment means performing many tasks that fall under the rubric "keeping the business going," and that can't be billed for. Marketing efforts, billing, research, bookkeeping, building or maintaining your databases, staying current on news related to your niche and your clients' businesses—all are important, to be sure, but none billable. Most VAs we've asked tell us that for every 10 hours they bill, they work one to one and a half non-billable hours managing their business. Keep this in mind as you imagine how your own VA business will look.

As a final word on finances, expect the unexpected. Surprises can be good or bad, and though we sincerely hope you'll have plenty of the former, we advise you to plan for the latter. The pleasant surprises will then be that much more pleasant, and the others that much less stressful.

Lifestyle Considerations

Successful entrepreneurs live in a world of possibility, it's true, but they face demands in the world of reality. Self-employment and entrepreneurship always have a direct and often profound impact on the businessperson's lifestyle—how we live, and want to live—and a VA business is no different.

Your "lifestyle preferences" embrace what you value as an individual: who you are, who you aspire to be, the priorities in your life, and the things that guide and motivate you. You'll need to take a careful, candid look at your personal profile and how you want to live if you want your VA business to be a good fit.

For example, if you love doing things spontaneously—if you're a "let's jump in the car and go to the beach!" type of person—you may find that running a business doesn't allow you much leeway. Or maybe you lead a lifestyle of eating out often, or rarely working weekends, or not thinking twice before buying that new coat or sofa or trading in your car. Or maybe you like to spend your summer weekends at your rented beach house and can't imagine a winter without a ski trip or two.

Certainly you can build your VA business to accommodate your need to "get up and go," and when you're successful you'll be able to indulge in material rewards again. But it will take work and good decision-making to get there, and you may have to tough it out for quite a while before the good old days can return. (On the other hand, you may find that the daily discipline required to keep a healthy balance sheet cures you of casual spending for good!)

And in the lifestyle context, think again about the time commitment you'll need to make to the business. (If you've ever had children, consider how surprised you were when you realized how much time they can take when they're babies. Young businesses are like that.) Contrary to popular belief, self-employment doesn't mean you'll have more free time. On the contrary, you'll usually have less, especially in the startup phase. Your lack of availability may be difficult for your family and friends (as we'll explore in more detail shortly). Likewise, you may go through periods where you yourself feel deprived of things or taken for granted.

Now is the time to set realistic goals and expectations for yourself, and help others in your life prepare for some of the changes that are sure to come with the launch of your business. We strongly recommend that you make a list of those things you just "can't live without," and ask those close to you for their input as well. This list—which may include items like going to the gym, attending your children's school and sports events, and "date night" with your spouse or significant other—will help you keep what is important to you in perspective as you design and ramp up your business.

Family Considerations

If you're not living alone—and for readers who are, we think you'll find some good thoughts here for future use— your business will be residing in your family's home, and this means that starting it should be a family decision.

Most of us wouldn't even consider changing the color of our living room walls without first discussing it with our family. After all, if you're thinking about painting the room violet, the other people who have to live with it have a right to an opinion, too! Now imagine how many larger adjustments can be involved in learning to "live with a business." In fact, as we mentioned earlier, it can be thought of as bringing a new baby into the home.

Consider this. Let's say your family feels that, home-wise, things are pretty much as they should be. They're comfortable with the routine of the household and the daily and evening and weekend activities, the general flow of things, and life, for them, is fine. You, however, though you're happy for them, feel unfulfilled. Something is missing from your life, and you think about it a lot. You yearn for something more, something to make you feel whole, more alive, and complete. So you launch a "little business." And you find it's just the thing you needed. Suddenly, you feel liberated and exhilarated and self-confident, and you're thrilled at the prospect of making something grow and prosper. In fact, you adore your new business and can't imagine how you ever got along without it. Your family, on the other hand, may not quite see it that way. From their point of view, this new "being" is competing with them for your time, your energy, your love and attention, and family finances. And if you aren't careful, your family may come to resent it.

If you have people in your life who depend on you for support—financially, psychologically, or for their general well-being—you must consider how your move to self-employment will affect them. Will your spouse or companion accept with patience and tolerance the interruptions that go with running a home-based business? When you toss and turn at night, worrying about the business, or get up and go to your office to check on some urgent phone call or e-mail, will you be met with complaints and sulking and a cold shoulder when you return to bed? If you need to tighten up the household budget while you get the business off the ground, will others in your home willingly accept the restrictions?

Women in particular, unfair though it may be, are often expected to keep the household running and attend to family needs and expectations regardless of whether they hold an outside job. So just imagine the "whole new way of looking at things" that will have to prevail in the house when the former core member of the family team has a new "baby"— her business—with all the care, attention, coddling and expenses that go with it! And there's one more little detail, and perhaps the most important one. Will you yourself be supported as you need to be when you take on the burden of your own company? Are the "significant others" in your life going to step into the breach when you need them, and offer you, too, a shoulder to lean or cry on?

Family members can not only be your primary source of indispensable encouragement, but are also meant to celebrate your successes with! Be sure to involve them in the decision to start a business in their home. To prepare the way for a smoother transition, sit down with them to discuss the kinds of changes you foresee. Now is the time to talk about the kind of help and support you feel you'll need and, if necessary, the redistribution of day-to-day household chores. Explain that there may be a period in which the budget will be a bit tighter than usual, and brainstorm together about how you can all work as a team to stretch the family dollars. You may be surprised at how many free or inexpensive entertainment opportunities you're overlooking every week. (A night out at a "spaghetti supper" fundraiser in your community, for example, can be much cheaper than going to the movies, and provide you with better quality time, to boot!)

Above all, open yourself to hearing their opinions and concerns, too. Really listen when they express their thoughts, reassuring them where appropriate and working to find mutually acceptable solutions. Remind them that the business is a vehicle for a better future for everyone, and make a point of sitting down with them regularly as a group as the business progresses. The idea of "family meetings" may sound hokey but, given the chance to share in a non-judgmental forum, most family members will do so and many problems can be solved or mitigated while they're still small.

Your New Boss: You!

We have all had good bosses, okay bosses, not-so-good bosses, and even the occasional "boss from hell." As you weigh the pros and cons of self-employment, consider carefully what kind of boss you'll be to yourself.

When co-author Chris was working as a VA, a reporter asked her to talk about how wonderful it was to be her own boss. This was her response:

There are times when I think that my new boss is a huge pain. Since joining the ranks of the self-employed, my new boss follows me everywhere, no matter where I go. I may be driving the car, or taking a shower, or drifting off to sleep at night, and she'll intrude: "So, when do you plan to launch that new section of the Website? Did you call that journalist in Singapore? Why didn't you? Did you remember to e-mail the accountant about the new e-commerce tax filings? How could you have forgotten that?" and so on.

To the best of my recollection, even my worst bosses have given me a little private time, and rarely did they hound me the way this new one does. Now my boss eats, sleeps, and showers with me, and criticizes every little thing I've left undone. She hangs around my house every Sunday, and catches me every time I try to leave work a few minutes early.

*My boss works me harder than anyone ever has,
and still she doesn't pay me on any kind of schedule.
Instead, she decides to issue me a check only when she
thinks the business can handle it. If it's been a bad
month, I may work like a slave and not even get a
"thank-you"!*

As we've emphasized, a new home-based business is very
similar to a new baby: It needs you, it shares your home, and
it demands your total devotion. You may even experience
"separation anxiety" when you're not with it—working. It may
sound unlikely or remote, as you sit comfortably reading, but
becoming obsessed with their business is a trap few entrepreneurs can avoid. Type "A" personalities are especially sus-
ceptible to what can easily become a ferocious attachment, so
if that describes you, you may need to work extra hard to
keep the business from running you and your family, instead
of the other way around!

Being a good boss will also require balancing self-praise
and self-discipline in the right measure. To accomplish this,
you'll need to:

✦ Keep yourself motivated to accomplish the tasks
you and your clients have set.

✦ Accept that although technically you have no
"boss," you're still accountable to your clients—
which can often make it seem that you have too
many bosses.

✦ Accept full accountability for your work.

✦ Know when to say "when"—to clients and yourself,
to avoid shoddy work, missed deadlines or burnout,
or alienating those close to you.

✦ Be flexible and resilient.

✦ Bolster your own spirits when nobody else is willing to be your cheerleader.

✦ Resist berating or punishing yourself when you fail to meet the goals you've set.

✦ Reward yourself for a job well done.

✦ Stay "tuned in" to your family and friends, as the best "pulse checkers" for how you're handling the pressures of self-employment.

If you can manage all of this, you'll have a much better chance of being a decent boss to yourself and balancing business and personal needs. But because the influence of the business can overtake even the most firm and well-intentioned VA, we suggest that you take a few moments to think of at least two core things you absolutely *will not allow to change* after you start your business. Write them down as statements that begin with, "I will never allow my business to interfere with...."

When you're done, tack the list to the wall in front of your desk, so you'll always be reminded of those two precious things. If you look at them three months from now and think they're no longer important, *that's probably the business speaking*, which means it's time to step back and get a grip on your priorities!

Readiness Assessments: Asking the "Tough Questions"

We've touched a bit on the "good, the bad, and the ugly" that you may encounter on the road to being a Virtual Assistant, and now it's time to take a more structured look at whether you yourself are ready to go out on your own.

Following are two self-assessments designed to help you evaluate your entrepreneurial profile in general, and more specifically your readiness to launch a VA business. Although they aren't scored—the questions aren't intended to yield "right" or "wrong" answers, but rather to help you gain insight and self-knowledge—you'll see that some questions are followed by a brief note explaining their importance.

The *Entrepreneurial Self-Assessment*, the first of the two, was developed to give you a sense of the attributes and behaviors that successful entrepreneurs share and to allow you to assess yourself in those areas.

Entrepreneurial Self-Assessment:
15 Questions Every Would-Be Entrepreneur Should Ask

1. Why do you want to go into business for yourself? List your top three reasons. Consider carefully whether these are compatible with your personal life goals.

2. What type of personal lifestyle do you want? Will your business allow for the hours and personal rewards that are important to you?

3. Are you reasonably confident that you can succeed? What is your confidence based upon?

   Your confidence in your ability to succeed is key. Successful entrepreneurs have doubts and fears in abundance, but an even higher degree of self-confidence. They compete with themselves as well as others and believe that success or failure lies within their personal control or influence.

4. Have you ever been in business before? If so, list why you feel you succeeded or failed. What did you learn that will help you this time around? How is your current situation different from the other(s)?

5. Do you want to work alone, or would you prefer to have a partner, associates, or employees? Are you gregarious, a "people person"?

    Most VAs, through choice but more often by necessity, work alone. You may have the company of your children or a pet, but is that enough for you? If you're gregarious, can you manage without frequent interaction with others? VAs do have the option of significant virtual contact through e-mail lists and online communities of other VAs and work-at-home entrepreneurs, and the social aspect will change as full-quality desktop audio and video evolve. Regardless of the tools, we encourage you to network often and to be attentive to your social needs generally. Otherwise, solitude can soon end up feeling more similar to "solitary confinement."

6. Do you have a mentor, or know where to find one?

    If you'd like the guidance of someone who has "been in the trenches" of self-employment, you may want to find a guru or mentor. Good candidates can be found via any of the various e-mail lists and other online groups that are available to VAs, or locally through the chamber of commerce, Rotary, or similar group. A word of advice, though, to keep the relationship healthy: Use sparingly. Respect your mentor's business or other obligations, and don't expect him or her to be at your disposal whenever needed.

7. Practically speaking, how do you want to spend your time each day? Does this fit with the requirements of the business you have in mind?

    Some aspiring VAs track everything they do for a week, to help get a "snapshot" of what their days really look like. This exercise may seem like a lot of work, but it can be an excellent means of determining where you can make room in your day for your business.

8. What are the financial risks of the business you are planning? Include your "worst-case scenario." Is it acceptable to everyone concerned?

9. What are the start-up costs? (At minimum, you must budget for a phone, fax, and high-end computer with good Internet access, preferably broadband.) Do you have practical ideas about how you can finance your business? List them.

    A worksheet for estimating startup costs has been included later in the book. See page 110.

10. Can you get along without a salary for an extended time? How long? Three months? Six months? How much will you need for your total monthly expenses pre-launch? Post-launch?

11. Ask yourself how you really feel about risk. Are you willing to take calculated but substantial chances?

    Are you a little scared? You should be! Starting a business is a bit like diving from the high board. Go to the local pool or swimming hole in the summer and, if there's a high diving board or cliff, you'll almost certainly see a band of kids gathered around it. Among them will be the "reckless risk-taker"—the kid who charges off the edge without looking down first to see what lies below. Then there's the "moderate risk-taker"—the one who looks over the edge to see if the first diver survived, surveys the water for hazards, then dives in. And finally, there's the "risk-averse"—the kid who watches everyone else dive and, though he or she wishes the courage were there, descends the ladder and enters the water from a safer place.

    It's the "moderate risk-taker" who has the greatest likelihood of succeeding in his or her business.

12. If you launch a business, will you have the support of your family and others close to you? To what degree?

13. Where would you want the business to be located? Is this feasible?

14. Are you able to set long-term goals? Can you stick to them despite adversity and discouragement, and in the absence of early rewards or success?

    How many unfinished projects do you have tucked away in a closet or laid out in your yard or garden? A few? A lot? Treat yourself as you'd treat your best clients: You'd move heaven and earth to help them achieve their long-term goals. Do the same for yourself, and you'll achieve so much more!

15. Your services will not sell themselves. Are you confident of your ability to market your skills? How do you feel about initiating contact with strangers, "pushing" your services, and "blowing your own horn"?

    Sales and marketing are, without a doubt, the hardest part of running any business. As a VA, you'll need to find a degree of comfort with "blowing your own horn," and talking up your services to your target market. The trick? Do only what you're good at, and you'll never have to question your right to brag.

Is a VA Business Right for You?

Your chances of having a successful VA business will go up dramatically if you have solid expertise, strong organizational and people skills, and a genuine interest in your field. The **VA Readiness Self-Assessment** will take you through a series of questions that will help you identify your relevant strengths and weaknesses and help you determine whether launching a VA business is a sound plan for you. As with the **Entrepreneurial Self-Assessment**, there are no right or wrong answers, but we've provided notes following some of the questions to help explain what we're getting at.

VA Readiness Self-Assessment: 20 Questions Every Would-Be VA Should Ask

1. Can you comfortably say "no" to non-critical interruptions that interfere with important activities and/or create work overload?

2. Do you take pride in your work?

   It's normal to have fluctuations in the quality of your work. No one hits their marks 100 percent of the time, and entrepreneurs themselves are famous for being dissatisfied with their accomplishments and always striving for improvement. What we're getting at here, as elsewhere in the questions, is consistency: *If you don't consistently take pride in your work, VAing (as self-employment) may not be the best option for you, because it requires that pride of effort be primarily "self-generated," coming before you receive the pat on the back.*

3. Do you have a generally positive and upbeat attitude?

   Chris's grandfather used to tell her, "Miss Chris, life is 50 percent attitude and the other half is attitude." An entrepreneur himself, and the father of 10 children, he often used such understated "Yankee pearls of wisdom" that, at the time, just sounded funny to the ears of a child.

   Only as she matured and pursued an entrepreneurial path herself did Chris truly understand the acuteness and value of his remarks. Successful entrepreneurs choose to go through life with a positive attitude, one of openness and assurance that they can make their dreams a reality. Attitude is a self-induced state of mind. Keep yours healthy, and your business, as an extension of yourself, is more likely to be healthy, too.

4. Can you communicate warmth and concerned interest effectively via phone and e-mail?

   Despite the influx of spam, Virtual Assistants still rely heavily on e-mail to communicate with potential and current clients. If you aren't yet adept at the fine art of effective business e-mail, you'll need to prioritize it to become a successful VA.

5. Do you have a solid record of establishing and achieving goals?

6. Are you willing to take responsibility for your actions even when the outcome is less than wonderful?

Is there anything more frustrating than having a service provider mess up a job you've given them, then deny it was their fault—or worse yet, imply it was your fault? For example, you've taken your trench coat to the dry cleaners, and when you go in to pick it up, you discover the belt is missing. When you ask the clerk or owner where it went, he tells you there was no belt with it when you dropped it off. What is the likelihood that you'll continue using that dry cleaner? Wouldn't you have been a little less irritated, and more likely to return, if he had accepted fault and attempted to make things right? Remember this when you (on the rare occasion!) deliver less-than-perfect work. Own up, make it right, and keep the client—who may also be so impressed that he tells his network just how exceptional you were.

7. Do you embrace change as a natural progression in business life, or do you thrive on predictability and continuity?

Working with multiple clients—each with a unique working style, personality, and range of workflow—is definitely a recipe for unpredictability. Although this doesn't have to equate to chaos, it can feel that way if you don't function well in a changing environment.

8. Do you consistently make effective decisions?

9. Do you deliver your services in a memorable way?

As you might guess, a good VA always strives for this. It makes clients remember you and eager to share their "great find" with colleagues and friends.

10. Can you accept constructive criticism without considering it a personal attack?

    Co-author Chris is the first to admit she has some serious issues with this. (Many people do—some are just better at hiding it than others!) Chris says, "Maybe it comes from growing up with five siblings, but when someone criticizes my work I perceive it as an attack, and am instinctively compelled to attack back. It took some doing, but over the years I've learned to overcome this gut reaction and accept creative criticism for what it is—simply input, and someone else's opinion on how the job could or should have been done. The bottom line is, if a client is paying you to do the job and wants to have something revised, it's their product— just do it. Even if you like your way better."

11. Are you a thinker, a doer—or a mixture of both?

    In an ideal world, every thinker would be paired with a "doer" and vice versa. Wouldn't it be great? The thinkers could sit back and think great thoughts and, when struck with a truly inspiring idea, they could simply beckon their doer to set about turning the thought into reality. Likewise, the doers would be eternally grateful to their thinkers for delighting them with endless "to do" lists!

    Humor aside, successful Virtual Assistants clearly need to be a mix of thinker and doer. In many cases, you'll act primarily as a "doer" for your clients but, because you'll also be running your own business, you'll need to be a thinker as well, to keep your business moving forward and strategically strong.

12. Are you the kind of person who easily establishes a rapport with a wide range of people?

13. Are you a good organizer of time? Tasks? Priorities? Details?

    To function well as a VA, you'll need to be. You'll be organizing your own time, tasks, and details as well as your clients'. If you have difficulty managing these things in your own life, you may want to think twice about taking on these tasks for others.

14. Do you possess basic computer and other technical skills needed to run the business?

15. How well do you know the Internet? Are you comfortable online?

16. Do others consider you dependable? Do you follow through on commitments?

    Words to live by: Say what you are going to do, then do it. Under-promise and over-deliver. Always finish what you start. Follow through and follow up. Whatever your philosophy, dependability is key to building a solid business.

17. If interrupted, can you easily return to the task you were working on?

18. Do you hold confidentiality of employer or client information in high regard?

    VA-client confidentiality is among the most fundamental principles of the industry. If you have trouble keeping confidences or secrets, you may encounter difficulties as a VA, not to mention legal liabilities if clients are harmed or perceive themselves so.

19. Do you understand the concept of "conflicts of interest" in handling multiple clients? (Some of your clients may directly or indirectly compete with each other, or have conflicting business goals. Likewise, current clients may be competitors of prospective clients.)

    When working with multiple clients, you'll have to be sensitive to the loyalties that are required and expected of you, and honor the trust that has been invested in you by each of your clients. Your first obligation is to existing clients, and you shouldn't accept clients whose relationship with you would either jeopardize or appear to jeopardize their interests. For example, if one of your clients is a real estate agent in Norwich, Connecticut, and a prospective client from a competitive firm in Norwich contacts you, it would generally be advisable to decline the second client.

Conflicts of interest and fiduciary duties are too complex to cover in detail here (and may be exceedingly elaborate in certain fields where many VA clients are found, most especially the legal and financial industries), but the Internet and your local library will have more than you need to answer most questions.

20. Do you have a desire to learn about your clients' businesses? Are you a quick learner?

One of the unique and most attractive aspects of being a VA is the stimulating diversity of intellectual and professional issues that comes from working with multiple clients, especially when they hail from various industries. A VA can wear many hats during the course of a single workday, and the opportunities for continuous learning and professional development are plentiful. Further, the more you learn about your clients' businesses and industries, the more valued and respected (and compensated) you become.

• • • • •

Now that you've completed the self-assessments, we hope you have a better idea of what it takes to succeed as a Virtual Assistant. If you're still not sure whether self-employment as a VA is the best option for you, go through this chapter again with a friend or family member whose judgment you trust, and who will be candid with you. Ask for their opinion. Compare notes. This exercise can be very revealing, since the people who are closest to us often see us more clearly than we see ourselves.

Spouse With a Mouse:

A Special Section to Share With Your Spouse or Significant Other

Note: This section is written primarily—though not exclusively—for your partner or significant other. We suggest that you read it through first, to get a feel for the material, and then share it. Once you've both reviewed it, take some time to discuss your concerns, goals, and expectations with each other, then complete the joint exercises you'll find included.

If the lines of communication are functioning well, your spouse or significant other has already told you that he or she is planning to launch a Virtual Assistance practice in the home you both share. The business, as a *houseguest*, is likeiy to be a bit of a mixed bag—quiet and unimposing at times, loud and intrusive at others—and it would be unfair for anyone to invite it into your home without preparing you beforehand. Earlier in this chapter, your partner learned about the realities of starting a home-based business. This section contains information for you individually (*the innocent bystander,* we might say) and for the two of you as a couple, to make sure you both have a realistic idea of the changes you're likely to see in your home and family life when the business "moves in."

When a partner decides to start a home-based business, most couples will struggle a bit with the same basic issues, such as:

✦   How to balance family, business, and personal needs.

✦ Coping with a lack of money or a tighter budget.

✦ Feeling as if the home is in the office rather than the other way around!

And as things proceed, you'll each face unique and varied challenges, determined in large part by your personalities, outlook, and lifestyles. Ultimately, however, the overriding theme of a home-based business should almost always be to provide a better life for your family. To achieve this goal, both partners must take the endeavor seriously, stay flexible and caring, and keep expectations realistic.

Myths and Realities

Many people dream of owning their own business, but too often these dreams are founded on myths and false assumptions, and they wind up disappointed or feeling betrayed. We'd like to dispel some of the myths involving home-based businesses and point out the contrasting realities behind them.

Myth #1: My Partner Will Have More Free Time

We can deflate this myth in one word: *wrong*. The reality is that, although your partner may enjoy more flexibility in scheduling his or her day, a young business can be extremely time-consuming, especially in the early phases.

Perhaps equally important, new businesses also demand a great deal of "mental energy." This means that sometimes when your partner appears to be available "in person," she still won't be entirely available mentally or emotionally, because the business or the needs of clients will be occupying her thoughts. (But don't be concerned; this is normal for every business owner. You should rather be concerned if she *isn't* preoccupied with the business.)

Myth #2: My Partner Won't Have a Boss to Answer To

We've all had terrible bosses at some time, but until someone has worked for himself, he hasn't met the worst boss he'll ever have. As bad as some of her bosses have been, your partner is about to start working for someone whose harsh gaze and critical voice she won't be able to flee. This new boss will follow her everywhere—the house, the car, the store—even the shower! Worse still, each of your partner's clients is another boss. So the reality is that your partner will have *many* bosses, and *all* of them will have to be served.

Myth #3: Our Home Will Be Cleaner and Better Organized

In most cases, a new business controls the owner long before the owner controls the business, so don't assume that time you spend at home is going to be well-organized. In the beginning, your partner will be devoting a lot of time to marketing and "beating the bushes" for clients. And once the clients are on board, they'll often be clamoring for his or her attention. There may be times when you come home and wonder, "What got done all day?" But hang in there—things *will* get better!

Myth #4: I'll Be Thrilled to Have My Partner Working at Home

Well...let's hope so! If your partner has been working outside the home, you might think at first that it's going to be great coming home to find her there. Can you picture it? A home-cooked meal and well-scrubbed children waiting for you in the doorway every night. A little slice of well-deserved paradise in your own four walls!

It might happen sometimes, but the truth is there'll be more occasions when you feel as if your home is in your partner's office rather than vice versa. And remember: If your partner has been working in the house all day, cooped up, you may find him or her at the door waiting to run out as you come in. "Glad you're home!" you may hear. "*You* take over!"

And Finally, Myth #5: We'll Get Rich!

Although self-employment does offer the possibility of unlimited income, most Virtual Assistants will not opt to work the 80-plus hours a week that might be required to get to "fat city." Money can be a great incentive for pursuing a business, but are you both willing to set aside so much else for those heavier pockets?

Few of us would say no to riches, but, as we said earlier, the business should be about making life better for your family *overall*, and that involves more than financial wealth alone.

Creating a "Family Vision Statement"

Suppose you decided it was time for your family to take a vacation, but you and your partner didn't bother to discuss where you wanted to go or what you wanted to do. So, each of you sets out to prepare for the trip that each has in mind. *You're* off to the store to pick up ropes and fittings for a rock-climbing expedition, and your *partner* is off to another store to buy beach towels and sunscreen for a restful week at the beach. Neither of you knows what the other has planned until one of you gets behind the steering wheel and heads off in the "wrong" direction.

Or to take the image further, if couples spend hours discussing and planning where they'd like to go for their limited two or three weeks of vacation each year, shouldn't they take a minute now and then to talk about where they'd like to go with the rest of their lives?

For most of us, it's easier to live our days "reactively" than to sit down and clarify our long-term "life goals," then get back up, fight the rudder over to where it ought to be, and live toward those goals. But reactive living is a trap, a meandering and depleting path that leaves us far short of where and who we could have been, of where and who we profoundly wanted to be. Having a "Family Vision Statement" (FVS) can make the difference between *surviving fate* and *navigating the future*.

An FVS that truly reflects the values of its writers (and the needs of their children) should function as a "blueprint" to guide the family's principal activities toward their collective Vision, or shared dream. The statement should be a brief but well-thought-out "proclamation" of the principles and goals of your family. And as the following examples demonstrate, these statements can be quite different from one family to the next.

"We envision our family healthy and debt-free with a home of our own, well-educated children, and money for a comfortable retirement."

• • • • •

"We will work together to build a life filled with love and laughter, honesty and caring, and will help each other achieve our dreams of home ownership, international travel, prosperity, and great adventure in our golden years."

• • • • •

"To create a life of balance in which family is given the time it deserves; work is given the time it requires; children are given the opportunities they merit, the wings to fly and the roots to stay steady; our bodies are given health for longevity and joyfulness; and love is given without limitation."

• • • • •

We strongly encourage you to work together to create an FVS that reflects your dreams. As you brainstorm about what should be included, consider the following:

✦ What kind of family do you want to become?

✦ What do you like most—and least—about your family now?

✦ How do you want to be perceived by others?

✦ What emotions or sentiments, and what code of conduct (character values), do you want to foster in your home?

✦ What makes you proud of your family?

Once you've written a statement that you're both pleased with, post it where you'll see it regularly—on the refrigerator door, bathroom mirror, computer monitor, nightstand, or wherever you'll have a prominent reminder of the course you've chosen for your Vision. This Vision can help marriages flourish and families move from stage to stage with greater ease, success and grace.

Assessing Your Values and Values Gaps

Healthy families require healthy foundations, built on the values we hold dear and aspire to live by. As with family visions, however, values are not a topic of frequent or even regular conversation in most households, yet their importance is indisputable. In the following exercise, you'll identify the six values that are most important to you as a family, determine how well you are living those values now, and set values goals for the future.

To begin, discuss your values with your partner and find six core values that you have in common and regard as important to your family. These might include:

family	spiritual	physical	social
intellectual	professional	material	emotional
parental	political	marital	educational

• • • • •

Once you've determined your core values, you'll be able to use the following exercise to identify the *gaps* that may exist between these values *as you aspire to live them* and the level at which *you are living them now*, consciously or unconsciously, in your everyday life. Identifying these "values gaps" relates directly to the home-based business: *It will help show you how to leverage the business to close them, or, in some cases, warn you of weak areas that, without proper planning, the business will exacerbate.*

The Values Pyramid

Following these instructions is a "Values Pyramid" (see page 82) with six bricks at the base. Review the following steps and then create your own Values Pyramid.

Step 1: Take the six values you selected and place them in the foundation bricks—one value per brick.

Step 2: Using the scale along the left side of the pyramid numbered one through 10 (10 being the highest), and keeping in mind the Family Vision Statement you created earlier, rate your *desired* (ideal) level in each of the values you just placed in the bricks at the base of the pyramid.

To illustrate, in the following sample the couple has placed the values "physical" and "spiritual" at the base of their pyramid. Ideally, they'd like to have good physical health, so they've set their "ideal" for physical at "8." Additionally, they feel a strong need for spirituality in their lives, so they have set that ideal at "10."

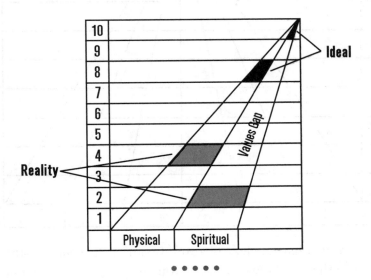

• • • • •

Step 3: Once you've determined your ideal level for each value, think about *where you are now* in terms of that value—how much of that value you are living or enacting in your day-to-day life. Now give this a rating, too, and mark it in each value area.

Referring again to the example, the couple assessed their current reality for "physical" as "4," and for "spiritual" they feel they are living a "2."

Family Values Pyramid Exercise

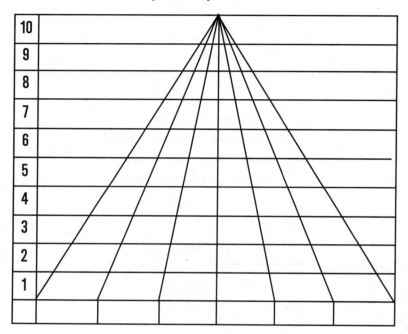

Now you have a clear picture of your "values gaps"—the distance that lies between where you and your family are now and where you would like to be. Only by closing these gaps can you move from your reality to your ideal and achieve the Vision you described in your FVS.

So how does this exercise pertain to launching a business in your home? To reiterate, the business will affect many areas of your life and will almost certainly play a role in either widening or narrowing your values gaps. Clearly, you want it to help *close* the gaps, if possible, and at the very least not make the gaps wider—taking you further from your values goals. But for this to occur, you need to plan now, *before* you launch the business.

For example, if the greatest gap you have is in the area of "family," you'll want to be especially careful that the business not be operated in a way that alienates the family. Long hours, lack of sleep, and cranky or overstressed attitudes would only widen the gap and undermine the quality and extent of the time you now spend together.

Thinking about how you want the business to develop within the framework of your core values will help assure your success as a family. Put another way, the business can be a powerful ally or a vexatious hindrance. A little planning now will help you keep friction down and headway up.

Family Meetings

One of the best ways to keep tabs on your progress toward your Family Vision is to hold periodic family meetings. Somehow, no matter how much time we spend with our families, we rarely take time out to focus on "how we are doing" overall, as a unit. Family meetings will give everyone a chance to speak their mind about how they are feeling or perceiving things in the "big picture"—including the business. And during these meetings it's important to encourage everyone to communicate in an open, non-critical, non-judgmental way, so each member feels that he or she can be open and honest with everyone else. We think you'll soon see that a little periodic "airing out" can do as much for a family as it does for sheets, clothes, and lungs.

The Family Plan

As a final step, we'd like to encourage you to discuss the following eight questions and really listen to each other's thoughts and responses. The keystone in any joint venture is mutual understanding and agreement.

1. How much are we willing to invest before the business becomes profitable?

2. Are we willing to take on credit card debt?

3. How are we going to pay the bills until the business is profitable?

4. When do we shut the business down if it is *not* profitable?

5. How many hours will the VA put into the business per week before he or she misses out on too much family time?

6. Can our marital commitment withstand additional challenges?

7. What sacrifices are we unwilling to make individually for the sake of business success?

8. How can we make sure we don't lose quality time with the children?

CHAPTER 4

Developing a "Service Menu" That You Can Live and Grow With

The term *professional satisfaction* may mean different things to different people, but most of us would probably agree that a key component is *enjoying what we do*. As a VA, you may find yourself working long hours and making many sacrifices to establish your practice and turn a profit, and even later on, when you can ease off a bit, the business will never be far from your thoughts. With something that plays such a dominant role in your life (not to mention your family's), it's critical that you like what you do.

"Liking what you do" includes being skilled at it and having people pay you to do it, which brings us to this chapter's theme: assessing your skills and determining your most marketable services, for the present and the future.

Unfortunately, many aspiring VAs take an overly narrow or modest approach to determining their skills generally and choosing the ones they'd like to offer to clients, and they forget to factor in other important matters such as values, interests, and the satisfaction they get (or don't) from performing the associated tasks. This not only limits their possibilities, but it may set the stage for reduced revenues, clients they have no chemistry with, unfulfilling work, and burnout. In this chapter you'll take a step-by-step approach to examining your work and life experiences, so you can assess your skills comprehensively and decide which of them would be best to offer to the marketplace.

Self-Knowledge: What Do You Value?

Although it's often overlooked in traditional business planning, being satisfied with your business often means understanding—and making business decisions that are consistent with—your values. *By identifying your values and projecting them into the business, you'll be more likely to create a business that will satisfy your needs on many levels.*

When we begin the process of identifying our values, we may often confuse them with goals. To help clarify, a goal is something to be achieved, an end result. A value is the vehicle that takes you *to* that goal. For example, "getting rich" or "retiring to a sailboat" is a goal, whereas "high income," "physical challenges," and "adventure" are core values. (And it's worth noting here that, ultimately, if we have lived by them, our core values also determine our legacy, our "life's work.")

2-Second Spotlight

"If It's Important to You, You'll Find a Way"
Name: Evy Williams

"My motto is, 'If you really want to do something, you'll find a way. If you don't, you'll find an excuse.'"

• • • • •

Your "Values Inventory"

The Values Inventory that follows is an exercise designed to help you identify and assess your most important values, so you can build a business that enacts and supports them.

Following is a list of 100 values that people commonly cite when they're asked what they care about most. Some are work-related, others are more personal. Review the list and select the 12 that are most important to you. (No need to rank them; for now just place a check mark in front of each.)

As you review the list, ask yourself these questions:

✦ What matters to me the most?

✦ What makes me feel happy and fulfilled?

✦ How would I define "success"?

Note: Feel free to add values that are important to you if they're not included here.

Values Inventory – Step 1

❑ Power/authority	❑ Advancement/promotion
❑ Community	❑ Competition
❑ Family time	❑ Economic return
❑ Working with numbers	❑ Economic security
❑ Merit	❑ Effectiveness
❑ Courage	❑ Fame
❑ Working with machines	❑ Friendships
❑ Helping society	❑ Honesty
❑ Working alone	❑ Frankness/candor
❑ Quality relationships	❑ Integrity
❑ Hobbies	❑ Intellectual standing/ status

- ❏ Public contact
- ❏ Knowledge/education
- ❏ Professionalism
- ❏ Recognition/status
- ❏ Personal growth
- ❏ Achievement
- ❏ Creative chaos
- ❏ Problem-solving
- ❏ Predictability
- ❏ Reputation
- ❏ Financial security
- ❏ Stability
- ❏ Sophistication
- ❏ Dignity
- ❏ Close relationships
- ❏ Intuition/empathy
- ❏ Flexibility
- ❏ Efficiency
- ❏ Money
- ❏ Excitement
- ❏ Helping other people
- ❏ Change and variety
- ❏ Cooperation/teamwork
- ❏ Involvement with people
- ❏ Decisiveness
- ❏ Routine work
- ❏ Ecological awareness
- ❏ Working with children

- ❏ Intellectual stimulation
- ❏ Leadership
- ❏ Moral fulfillment
- ❏ Orderliness/neatness
- ❏ Persuading others
- ❏ Physical challenge
- ❏ Humility
- ❏ Public attention
- ❏ Public service
- ❏ Responsibility
- ❏ Self-expression
- ❏ Self-respect
- ❏ Supervising others
- ❏ Detail/intricate work
- ❏ Influencing others
- ❏ Location
- ❏ Health
- ❏ Ethical practices
- ❏ Nature
- ❏ Fast pace
- ❏ Argument/debate
- ❏ High quality of product
- ❏ Independence
- ❏ Climate
- ❏ Loyalty
- ❏ Leadership
- ❏ Service
- ❏ Working with hands

- Personal development
- Physical work
- Creativity
- Management
- Prestige
- Challenging problems
- Security
- Travel
- Working under pressure
- Truth
- Solitude

- Autonomy
- Using the senses
- Privacy
- Material status
- Working with seniors
- Independence
- Serenity
- Freedom
- Mentoring/advising
- Wealth
- Social

Values Inventory – Step 2

Take a moment to transfer the 12 values you've selected to the lines here.

_____

_____

_____

_____

_____

_____

_____

_____

_____

_____

_____

_____

Values Inventory – Step 3

Now, suppose you had to squeeze these values through a funnel that would allow only six to come out on the other side. Which of these 12 values would you choose? List these here.

_____

_____

_____

_____

_____

_____

• • • • •

Congratulations! You've just identified the six core values that are most important to you! These values should be at the center of your planning as you proceed toward developing the best VA practice for you.

Getting Your Bearings: The Personal Values Statement (PVS)

Now that you've identified your core values, it's time to write a Personal Values Statement (PVS), converting the essence of what's important to you into clear, succinct sentences.

The PVS is intended to serve as a compass for your goals and career-development preferences. Usually, it consists of a series of "I" statements that define, in the context of life and work or business, the best of the person you are and the best of the person you *want to be*. An honest PVS will help you achieve and maintain consistency in the way you make work-life decisions.

Every PVS is unique, because the "P" stands for Personal—you. The two PVS examples that follow were written by different people who have picked the same six values: *money, service, dignity, integrity, wisdom,* and *challenging problems.* The format is simple: First comes a short statement about how the writer intends to adhere to his or her core values, followed by a statement about the effect that this action will likely have on the business.

Though the authors of these sample statements have identified the same core values, this is where the similarities in their PVSs end. As you read them, notice how identical values can be interpreted in dramatically different ways, and with varying career goals in view. Bear in mind as you read them that there are no "right" or "wrong" values, and that each of us will combine values and interpretations that are unique to our individual lives.

Sample PVS 1 was written by a 45-year old man who has decided that some of the career choices he has made over the years, though they've provided a healthy income, have ultimately demanded too much of his personal life. You will see how his PVS reflects his feelings about the past and his hopes for the future.

Sample PVS 2 was written by a 25-year-old woman who is living in a location where "everyone seems to have more" than she does. At this time and place in her life, she seeks prestige and material outcomes most of all. As with the first sample, you'll see how she has crafted statements that "cut to the chase," rendering a clear picture of what she wants to accomplish through her business.

Sample PVS 1

MONEY

Money is my servant, not my master. I will seek to keep myself free of debts and pay obligations as soon as possible. I will strive to increase my income, but not by increasing my workload to the point where I neglect my family.

(*Effect on business: As a person who values money, but does not place it before other important values, I am less likely to feel I must "endure" projects that pay well but are unfulfilling for me. Rather, I will choose clients and tasks that bring me satisfaction.*)

SERVICE

I will strive for excellence in anticipating and responding to the requirements of the people I serve.

(*Effect on business: By serving my clients well, I will also serve my business well. Providing excellent service to clients will allow me to feel proud of my work, while helping me gain and keep my clients' respect. Thus I will have greater opportunities for long-term relationships and secure valuable referrals as well.*)

DIGNITY

I will recognize and affirm each and every person as a unique individual worthy of respect, understanding, and compassion. Their dignity and mine are inseparable.

(*Effect on business: Dignity is a quiet confidence, not proud or bullying, but a knowing of one's priorities and values and worth. As a person who possesses and grants dignity, I am fully aware that the success of one is the success of all—making me an invaluable and respected partner to my clients.*)

INTEGRITY

I will build each relationship on honesty and trust, delivering on my promises and treating everyone fairly.

(Effect on business: As a person of integrity I will be well-respected by my peers and clients alike. As a result, they will be confident and comfortable in recommending me to their colleagues, customers, partners, and friends.)

WISDOM

I will share ideas and insights, and seek knowledge to act meaningfully, productively, and responsibly.

(Effect on business: By honoring this value, I will increase my expertise and professionalism and will be more likely to be esteemed as a valuable asset by my clients.)

CHALLENGING PROBLEMS

I will choose to be more of a product of my decisions than of my conditions. I will not allow irrelevant facts or negative events in the past determine how I respond to challenges and overcome hurdles. Rather, I will help my clients and myself by seeking optimal solutions for the situation at hand.

(Effect on business: I will be a problem-solver rather than someone who shies away from difficult situations or reacts to them in a conventional or routine manner. My clients will recognize me as a creative and effective problem-solver and my business will thrive.)

SAMPLE PVS 2

MONEY

Money, and the status and material benefits that come with it, are very important to me. I will do whatever I must to ensure a lifestyle that I will be content with.

(Effect on business: As a person who understands the value of money and the things it can bring, I am prepared to work long hours and commit myself fully to my work. I am also prepared to accept assignments and tasks I do not care for, as long as I am well compensated for my efforts.)

SERVICE

I will strive to serve my clients according to the standards they expect of me.

(Effect on business: By serving my clients well, I will earn their confidence and will likely be referred to their colleagues, thereby increasing my billable hours.)

DIGNITY

I will treat others as I want to be treated myself: with dignity and respect.

(Effect on business: By treating others with dignity, I will earn the respect of my clients. Through this, my clients will be more likely to speak well of me to others and, through this positive word of mouth, help me build a larger client base.)

INTEGRITY

I will be honest in my work relationships and will strive to treat everyone fairly regardless of my personal feelings toward them.

(Effect on business: As a person of integrity, I will earn the esteem and trust of my clients, which will help insure continuing workflow.)

WISDOM

I will make use of the wisdom and knowledge I have gained in my work experience to perform with excellence in my business.

(Effect on business: By employing my accumulated knowledge in my daily tasks, I will demonstrate to my clients my value to their businesses, thereby increasing the probability of long and profitable relationships.)

CHALLENGING PROBLEMS

I enjoy facing challenging problems and will do so in my work with the focus and determination I need to achieve effective solutions.

(Effect on business: My name will be the first one that clients think of when challenging problems arise, and I will become a more appreciated and sought-after professional with each success.)

• • • • •

Now that you've identified your six core values and seen two examples of PVSs, it's time to develop your own—unique to you. But be advised, it isn't an easy exercise: Values are something we aspire to live by but rarely discuss with others or even think about in detail. Accordingly, some people find it useful to work on their PVS over the course of several days, rather than trying to cram it all into one sitting.

Self-Knowledge: What Are Your Interests?

"Interests"—areas that grab your attention and stir your enthusiasm—are usually closely related to your values and often spark or support skill development. Because interests are usually embedded in the activities we find the most enjoyable or fulfilling, they're often easy to identify.

Think about the recurring themes in your life: ways you've spent your free time, things you daydream about, the kinds of books you like to read, pastimes or hobbies you've returned to regularly, consistent choices, and so on. Such themes usually indicate a strong interest. Now imagine building a business that you're hoping will last for a long time, but that *doesn't* include any of your interests. Sound enticing? Or deathly boring? *The importance of considering your interests when you're planning your VA practice should not be underestimated!*

Your "Interests Inventory"

The following exercise will help you begin to clarify what really engages you, and what "leaves you cold." As you consider the questions, take your time, be as honest as you can (for example, don't say "I have a good imagination" or "I like group activities" only because you feel you should), and write out your answers.

1. If you had some time to spare, what would you do?

2. What repeatedly or frequently arouses your curiosity, or triggers your enthusiasm?

3. What do you enjoy doing most? What, in particular, pleases you about this activity?

4. What types of activities generally do you enjoy participating in? Why?

5. Do you prefer—or dislike—group or solo activities? Why? (Include work, social activities, and sports.)

6. What are your favorite hobbies?

7. What courses did you enjoy most, and least, in school?

8. When you fantasize about a career, what do you see yourself doing? Include details.

9. What do you really dislike doing or find boring or mundane?

10. Do you see yourself as a practical person? Give examples.

11. Are you artistic? If so, how does your artistic side express itself?

12. Are you good at math and science?

13. Do you like to solve problems or discover things? (Think of examples and what they involved.)

14. Do you have a good imagination? If so, how does it express itself?

15. Do you like reading, music, art, or theater? Why?

16. Are you a great organizer or administrator?

17. Do you consider yourself articulate? Orally, or only in writing?

18. Do you like to influence others? If so, to take what kinds of action?

19. Do you enjoy responsibility, achievement, and working toward goals?

20. Do you enjoy following processes and meeting standards?

● ● ● ● ●

Again, as you sift through and weigh your answers, look for recurring themes, veins, and patterns—the melody and the harmony in the song. And don't forget to ask family members and friends for their input, too. Sometimes our view of the forest is obscured by the trees!

Self-Knowledge: What Are Your Skills and Abilities?

Now that you have a better idea of your values and interests, it's time to turn to your abilities and skills. Virtual Assistants who have a firm grasp of these, and who can describe them succinctly to prospective clients, are much more likely to have a satisfying, enjoyable, and sustainable practice.

In the exercises that follow, we'll be asking you to identify and list your abilities and skills, so let's pause briefly for a moment to note the difference between the two. In a nutshell, an ability might be thought of as a natural talent or capacity to do something, and the skill is the "something"—the end activity. For example, you may have a strong creative *ability* that contributes to your *skills* as a graphic designer.

Developing a list of your abilities and skills can help you clarify your strengths, boost your confidence, spark your strategic thinking, and arrive at a service menu that's a good fit for you. For the first step, we've provided a list of abilities and related "thought-starters" that will help you get the ideas flowing. Then you'll be ready to inventory your skills and marketable services for your service menu.

As you review the Abilities Checklist and reflect on your experience, err on the side of over-inclusion. Don't limit yourself to the present or near-past, but go back at least as far as your high school years, and don't be modest. As adults, we often understate our abilities for fear of being criticized or embarrassed, but don't let that hinder you here. Giving your mind free rein may help you identify abilities that you had forgotten you had!

Finally, don't worry if some of the abilities you check off can't be used in a virtual environment. They're still pieces in the mosaic of the practice that suits you best, and you'll be taking them into account in a later chapter when we help you identify your best business niche and target markets.

Your "Abilities Checklist"

- ❏ Hand coordination
- ❏ Working with machines
- ❏ Working with nature
- ❏ Working with animals
- ❏ Working with children
- ❏ Problem solving
- ❏ Analysis, logic
- ❏ Evaluate, assess
- ❏ Research, investigate
- ❏ Conceive
- ❏ Discover
- ❏ Study, observe
- ❏ Conceptualize
- ❏ Entertain, perform
- ❏ Intuition, insight
- ❏ Artistic ability
- ❏ Creativity, imagination
- ❏ Write
- ❏ Critique
- ❏ Care, heal
- ❏ Implement
- ❏ Translate
- ❏ Planning events, organization
- ❏ Mediate
- ❏ Instruct, teach

- ❏ Administer
- ❏ Advise, influence
- ❏ Manage, direct, delegate
- ❏ Motivate
- ❏ Initiate, anticipate
- ❏ Convince, persuade
- ❏ Negotiate
- ❏ Advocate, debate
- ❏ Demonstrate
- ❏ Financial, account
- ❏ Attention to detail
- ❏ Calculate, compute
- ❏ Appraise, estimate
- ❏ Monitor
- ❏ Coordinate
- ❏ Organize, arrange
- ❏ Counsel, coach
- ❏ Comfort, serve
- ❏ Guide
- ❏ Prioritize
- ❏ Promote change
- ❏ Integrate
- ❏ Decide
- ❏ Compare
- ❏ Examine

Now that you've identified your core values, interests, and abilities, it's time to move on to what you'll actually be offering to clients in your VA practice: the service menu. Our goal? To help you establish a business that will allow you to *live your values, indulge your interests,* and *use your skills.*

Developing Your "Service Menu"

Now you're ready to take an inventory of your job skills and determine your level of expertise and satisfaction in performing each. The list of services we've included here isn't meant to be definitive, but it is a good representation of what other VAs are offering. If there are others you'd like to provide, just note and rank them on a separate sheet and keep it handy for later.

To complete the exercise, first review the list of services on pages 102–106 and place a check in the column to the right that best describes your skill and satisfaction level in performing each.

Next, assess your responses and divide them as follows:

High Skill Level + High Satisfaction

These are the areas you'll definitely want to include in your ideal practice. If you love what you're doing, you'll be much more likely to work hard at it and stick with it through the ups and downs of your business. Just as importantly, you'll be genuinely enthusiastic about what you do—which will be duly noted and appreciated by both current and prospective clients.

Highlight these services by placing a check in the "**offer**" column to the left of each.

Moderate Skill Level + High Satisfaction

Given your "less than expert" skill level, you shouldn't offer these services right away, for sub-optimal performance can not only lose you clients but damage your reputation.

However, because you enjoy doing them, you'll likely want to add them to your service menu at a later date—after you're gained proficiency and can deliver stellar work. Indicate these services by placing a check in the "**learn/ add**" column to the left of each.

High Skill Level + Low Satisfaction

Although you can probably earn some money delivering services in this category, it's a desperate option, and you should avoid it if you possibly can. There's plenty of boring work in most places if people want to look for it, but do you really want to build a business around it? And why go the risky route of entrepreneurship just to arrive at work you don't like?

However, if you find after due reflection that the financial rewards outweigh the dissatisfaction, consider offering these services in a limited capacity so you can balance them with other services that you enjoy.

High Skill Level + Moderate Satisfaction

If you have a high skill level but the work is only moderately satisfying, keep this service in reserve, to bring on board if your menu or revenues are thin. Though you won't want to found a business on work that leaves you lukewarm, we all need to be pragmatic, and if your situation requires it you can offer these services for a limited time and to limited clients while you develop workflow and a client base that keep you truly happy.

• • • • •

You now have a useful snapshot of what you can offer your clients immediately, and a map of what to add in the future. Now give yourself a pat on the back! The self-discovery process, though difficult, is critical to planning and building a successful VA practice, to reward and delight you in the many years ahead.

Learn/ Add	Offer	Service	High Skill Level	Moderate Skill Level	Low Skill Level	High Satisfaction	Moderate Satisfaction	Low Satisfaction
		Academic Writing						
		Accounting Services						
		Audiovisual Production						
		Benefits & Payroll Services						
		Bookkeeping						
		Business Coaching						
		Business Plan Writing						
		Business Writing						
		CAD						
		Collection Services						
		Competitive Research						
		Computer Hardware Design Services						
		Computer Programming Services						
		Concierge Services						
		Construction Consultation & Design						
		Consulting						
		Corporate Training & Development						
		Database Management						

Learn/ Add	Offer	Service	High Skill Level	Moderate Skill Level	Low Skill Level	High Satisfaction	Moderate Satisfaction	Low Satisfaction
		Desktop Publishing						
		Dictation & Court Transcription Services						
		Document OCR/ Scanning						
		Drafting						
		Editing/Proofreading						
		Engineering Consultant						
		Entertainment Industry Support						
		Event Planning						
		Expertise in Non-U.S. Markets						
		File Conversion						
		Fundraising						
		Genealogy Services						
		General Transcription						
		Ghostwriter						
		Government Procurement						
		Grant Proposals						
		Graphic Design						
		Graphic Scanning						

Learn/ Add	Offer	Service	High Skill Level	Moderate Skill Level	Low Skill Level	High Satisfaction	Moderate Satisfaction	Low Satisfaction
		Growth Advisory Services						
		HR Expertise						
		Internet Research						
		Interpreting						
		Import/Export Support						
		Intranet Development/ Management						
		Journalist (Freelance)						
		Lecturer/Facilitator (Online)						
		Legal "Secretarial"						
		Legal Transcription						
		Literary Agent						
		Litigation Support						
		Live Phone Answering for Clients						
		Mailing Services						
		Manufacturing Consultant						
		Marketing/Advertising						
		Market Research						

Learn/ Add	Offer	Service	High Skill Level	Moderate Skill Level	Low Skill Level	High Satisfaction	Moderate Satisfaction	Low Satisfaction
		Medical Transcription						
		Multilingual						
		Multimedia Presentation						
		Nonprofit Support Services						
		Nursing-Related Services						
		Office Management						
		Online Tutoring/ Teaching						
		Paralegal Services						
		Payroll Services						
		Phone-in Transcription						
		Private Investigation Support						
		Programming						
		Public Relations						
		Realtor Support						
		Research & Information Retrieval						
		Resume Writing						

Learn/ Add	Offer	Service	High Skill Level	Moderate Skill Level	Low Skill Level	High Satisfaction	Moderate Satisfaction	Low Satisfaction
		Software Support Services						
		Spreadsheets						
		Statements/Billing						
		Systems Management						
		Talent/Booking Services						
		Technical Support (Hardware)						
		Technical Writing/ Editing						
		Translating Services						
		Travel & Reservation Services						
		Virtual Outsourcing Project Mgr.						
		Voice Services (Greetings, Events)						
		Voice mail for Clients						
		Website Design						
		Word Processing						
		Writing & Editorial Services						

CHAPTER 5

Estimating Costs and Setting Fees

We'd live in a wonderful world if being a great VA was all you needed to pay the bills, but the fact is that you have to be a good businessperson as well. In this chapter, you'll put your business instincts to the test as you tackle two of the slipperier tasks VAs have to handle: estimating costs and setting fees.

Projecting Your Expenses

You'll need to get a grip on your estimated expenses before you can begin thinking about your fees. But the good news is that the costs of starting and maintaining a VA practice are usually quite modest and, if you're like most new VAs, much of the equipment and software you'll need to launch will already be on hand.

The minimum package generally includes the following:

✦ A personal computer with maximum affordable memory.

✦ A high-speed Internet connection (if dial-up, a dedicated line is best).

+ A telephone with voice mail or an answering machine.

+ A fax machine or computer-based fax application.

+ Basic "office suite" software applications (Microsoft, Corel, Lotus).

+ Anti-virus software, such as McAfee or Norton.

If you intend to offer services that require specialized equipment or software, be sure to figure in their cost, too. For example, for graphics production you may need Adobe Illustrator or Paint Shop Pro, and desktop publishing may require Adobe Pagemaker or Microsoft Publisher. Some of these programs can be quite pricey, so if you can squeak by without them for a while, do so, and purchase them later out of business revenues, rather than with your credit card. (For those unfamiliar with this approach, it's called *bootstrapping*—financing growth from revenue, as you go. This helps minimize or eliminate debt, the greatest temptation for new entrepreneurs. Whenever you can, *bootstrap, bootstrap, bootstrap!*)

2-Second Spotlight

Keeping Expenses Down
Name: Evy Williams

"I save money by using my cell phone as my business phone. This way I am always accessible, and I don't have to get a separate business line. (Fortunately, I have an outstanding phone plan.)

I also use a free incoming fax service, and save my fax machine for the few outgoing faxes I send.

My children also help me do things such as fold flyers, stuff envelopes, and apply stamps to mailings. To reward them, I take them out for lunch or a similar treat. I also paid my oldest daughter to enter information into a database for me, so I could access it conveniently for marketing purposes."

• • • • •

We've included a worksheet on page 110 to help you estimate your startup costs and recurring monthly expenses, so you can get a better picture of how much revenue the business will have to generate to cover your outflow. (It's all right to "ballpark" costs at this stage, as you have no operational history to base your numbers on.) These projections will also give you a starting point for setting your fees.

A final note: If you're married or otherwise sharing expenses, be sure to get your partner's input as well, because your projected costs may also involve the household finances.

Picking Your "Salary"

Besides your projected expenses, there are other factors to consider when setting your fee schedule. Prominent among them is the question of how much will you pay yourself.

Although it's not likely you'll be drawing a regular "salary" when your business is in the development stages, you should plan to pay yourself a reasonable wage regularly as soon as your cash flow permits. In your own unique circumstances, how much should a reasonable "salary" be? As you weigh the question, consider the following aspects:

✦ The value of your service to your prospective clients.

Startup Cost and Recurring Expense Estimate Worksheet

Item	One-Time Startup Cost	Recurring Monthly Cost
Fixtures and equipment	_____	
Remodeling/Decorating	_____	
Installation of Fixtures/Equip.	_____	
Domain Registration	_____	
Stationery	_____	
Office Supplies/Starting Inventory	_____	
Phone Line Installation Fees	_____	
Legal/Accounting Fees	_____	
Licenses and Permits (if needed)	_____	
Advertising of Opening	_____	
Software	_____	
Opening Cash	_____	
Other	_____	
Rent (if applicable)		_____
Advertising		_____
Postage/Freight		_____
Office Supplies		_____
Telephone		_____
Utilities		_____
Insurance		_____
Taxes		_____
Maintenance		_____
Legal/Professional Fees		_____
Internet Connection Charges		_____
Domain Hosting Fee		_____
Other		_____
TOTALS	_____	_____

✦ The fact that you're selling a customized solution, not a commodity.

✦ Your expertise in your field.

✦ The complexity of the work you'll be doing.

✦ How the quality of your prospective services compares with your competitors'.

If you're still not sure where to begin or how to balance things out, the free, easy-to-use "Salary Wizard" at Salary.com (*www.salary.com*) can give you a working idea of what you might expect to be paid if you were an employee. Keep in mind that the salaries provided in their "basic" report (the free option) assume full-time employment, so you'll need to prorate those figures according to how many hours per week you intend to work.

Setting Your Hours

VAs vary greatly in the number of hours they work, with some preferring less than 10 hours per week, and others shooting for 30 or more. (We can say that the majority of VAs we work with express a preference for a part-time schedule, leaving them time for other duties and priorities.) It's really a question of your unique needs, goals, and circumstances. However, as you consider the question, you'll want to bear in mind that, as we mentioned earlier, not all working hours are "billable hours."

Most established VAs report that their business week consists of billable hours plus roughly 15 percent. In other words, a VA who is billing 30 hours per week is actually working 15 percent (4.5 hours) over that, or 34.5 hours. During those extra hours, the VA may be taking care of accounts payable, billing, or the many other duties that come with running a business, such as marketing to new clients and keeping current relationships strong. (Here we're reminded of a top producing car salesman we read about who spent only a fraction of his time actually "on the floor" selling cars. Much more of his time, and money, he said, was spent writing birthday cards, Bar Mitzvah notes, wedding and birth congratulations, funeral condolences, and college graduation notes.)

Naturally, because you're just starting out and don't have your first clients yet, your billable to non-billable ratio will be dramatically different: 100 percent of your time will be devoted to the launching and marketing of your business.

Establishing Your Fees

We've talked a bit about the "salary" you'd like, but there are many other variables that can go into the question of fees—which is why economists have filled the halls of university libraries with treatises on the subject. We obviously don't need to go into that kind of detail here, but a brief discussion as you prepare to develop your own fee schedule can only help you in the early stages, and later too when you adjust your fees to match dynamic conditions in your practice.

To get a sense of what a "reasonable" fee is, it helps to understand how the viewpoints of buyer and seller differ when it comes to pricing, and how VAs differ from other service providers.

For the buyer-client, the "right" price may be a function of need, perceived value of the service offered, and the pricing and availability of comparable services in the marketplace. For the seller-VA—who, unlike other independent professionals such as lawyers, dentists, consultants, and so on, may only want to work a limited number of hours per week, to supplement a spouse's or companion's income—the "right" price will include such considerations as the aforementioned weekly schedule and "ideal" salary, competitor pricing, the target client base, overhead (including the cost of continuing education or professional development), family financial objectives, and whether the VA intends to subcontract work to other VAs or similar service providers.

We can't tell you what your fees ought to be, but we can tell you how some of the caveats in fee-setting play out. Let's take some examples from our VA trainings. There, we are often asked, "Why can't I just see what everybody else is charging and charge less? People are always shopping for the lowest price. And then I wouldn't have to market so hard." Well, set your fees too low, and several things may happen: You can be flooded with more business than you can handle, causing disappointed clients and poor word of mouth; you can work long hours and still not make enough to cover your expenses and make a profit; and you can be saddled with a "cut-rate" image in the marketplace that you didn't want and will have a tough time changing.

"OK," the student may say. "I'll set them high and position myself on the upper end. I'll be the Rolls-Royce of the market." Maybe. But keep in mind that the typical VA client is a small business—a micro-enterprise—looking to keep costs down, or an independent professional such as the VA herself. So the question arises: When was the last time *you* bought a Rolls-Royce?

Similarly, if your fees don't take into account—or inadequately serve—the financial objectives of the couple or family, you can quickly be on a course to disappointment and failure. And don't underestimate the emotional side here. After all, as we've mentioned before and will again, the significant others in the picture, from their point of view, are making a major sacrifice when you go into business and start tending the new entity—they're "giving you up." There won't be many happy campers left at the kitchen table if you disappear into a basement office and reemerge 12 months later, exhausted though you may be, with much less to show for it than you promised—or they expected.

"Running the Numbers": A Helpful Formula for Fees

To give you another thought-starting tool as you work on your fees, we've devised a simple formula that takes your projected expenses, salary, and hours, adds in some profit, and yields an hourly rate.

A. Add your annual expenses to your annual "salary."

B. Multiply the sum by 15 percent (or whatever profit margin you'd like to make).

C. Add "A" to "B."

D. Divide "C" by your projected annual billable hours.

In the following example, the VA has determined that her annual overhead (expenses associated with running her business) will be $4,000, her salary will be $30,000, and she'll be billing 30 hours per week and working 48 weeks (1,440 hours) per year.

A. $30,000 + $4,000 = $34,000

B. $34,000 × 15% (profit margin) = $5,100

C. $34,000 + $5,100 = $39,100

D. $39,100 / 1,440 hours = $27.15 per hour

As we say, this final figure doesn't have to be definitive, but at least you have a simple way to arrive at a starting point.

Our Annual Fee Survey: What Are Other VAs Charging?

Now that you have a better sense of what your fees might be, we suggest you do some competitive research and see what other VAs are charging for the services you'd like to offer. A simple search with your favorite search engine will turn up thousands of VA Websites. Burrow in a bit to see your colleagues' rates, payment terms, service menu, and other details. This will be useful not only for your fee calculations, but also as you create your own Website and marketing materials.

If you want to sell to local businesses, your online research can be coupled with local sources. For example, search the classified ads in your local paper to see if any of the "help wanted" listings include salary information. It can also be helpful to check the rates that local temporary agencies are charging businesses, to see what local companies are accustomed to paying for contingency or "as-needed" workers.

VA industry fee surveys, which are sometimes available to the public online or in print, can obviously be an excellent reference as well. For our own part, each year we conduct our "Work Practices & Fee Survey" by soliciting input from the largest group of VAs in the world, and our 2004/2005 survey fee results follow for your review. (Here, our legal eagles have advised us to add that neither we nor our company, Staffcentrix, recommend, advise, or endorse the implementation of any fee, fee structure, or billing increment practice. The sole purpose of this information is to provide you with additional background on the Virtual Assistant industry.)

2004/2005 Fee Survey Results
(All fees are hourly unless otherwise noted.)

Service	Average Fee ($)
Academic Writing	32
Accounting Services	34
Audio Visual Production	40
Business Coaching	50
Business Plan Writing	600/project
Business Writing	35
Collection Services	31
Competitive Research	33
Concierge Services	33
Data Entry	.25/other
Database Management	39
Desktop Publishing	29
Document OCR/Scanning	3/page
Editing/Proofreading	33
Entertainment Industry	30
Event Planning	40
File Conversion	33
Fundraising	30
General Transcription	30
Government Procurement Expertise	45
Grant Proposals	50
Graphic Design	35
Graphic Scanning	28
HR Expertise	45
Insurance Broker/Agent Support	33
Internet Research	33
Interpreting	42
Import/Export Support	35

Service	Average Fee ($)
Intranet Development/Management	55
Legal "Secretarial"	40
Legal Transcription	35
Litigation Support	35
Live Phone Answering for Clients	28
Mailing Services	25
Marketing/Advertising	35
Market Research	35
Medical Transcription	35 or .05/word
Multimedia Presentation	47
Nonprofit Support Services	30
Office Management	36
Paralegal Services	35
Payroll Services	34
Phone-in Transcription	32
Private Investigation Support	30
Programming	69
Public Relations	48
Real Estate – Transaction Management	250/project
Realtor Support	33
Resume Writing	38
Spreadsheets	32
Statements/Billing	30
Systems Management	50
Technical Writing/Editing	45
Translating Services	39
Voice Services (Greetings, Events)	50
Website Design	40
Word Processing	29

To Bend or Not to Bend?

Once you've set your fees, will you stick to them, or will you bend? All VAs can tell you stories about clients who wanted a reduced rate—indeed, many clients feel "duty bound" to negotiate. But this is your business, not theirs. You call the shots. How will you respond?

In our view, it pays to be firm, but not always—sometimes bending can be better. Co-author Chris recalls an early client who needed assistance desperately, but because her business was new she was going to have a hard time paying the quoted rate. This particular client had an amazing Rolodex, and it was agreed that Chris would lower the fee in exchange for some "selective" name-dropping by the client. The result was a "win-win": The client got the support she needed to grow her business at a rate that didn't bankrupt her, Chris still got decent revenue for effort, and the referrals Chris received from the client more than made up for the discount she gave.

In other cases, lowering your rate or underbidding on a job may enable you to show a desirable client just how valuable you can be or help you land a "flagship" name for your client list. (Just be sure it's clearly understood that the lower figure is *confidential* and *introductory*—confidential because you don't want to have to work for all the world at the same low rate, and introductory to avoid the stickiness of trying to negotiate the fee upward at a later date.)

If you decide to stand firm on your fees, keep these tips in mind when the other client seeks to negotiate:

✦ **It's okay to say no!** We all hate to tell our clients no, but sometimes it's the only prudent reply.

✦ **Be firm, but polite, and respond promptly.** Delay may be perceived by the client as room for more negotiation.

✦ **Have good reasons for standing firm, and be prepared to explain them.** For example: *"The rates you've proposed don't allow me to cover the expenses of doing business"* or *"I can't deliver the high-quality results that you expect and that I demand of myself, if I try to compress the work to stay within the budget you're suggesting."*

✦ **Prepare a counterproposal.** Though the client's terms may not be acceptable, don't neglect workable alternatives. The more ideas you can present for the client's consideration, the better!

And no matter how the negotiations run, remember: *"It's only business."* If discussions take a turn for the worse, politely bring them to a close and invite the client to call back if his or her needs or circumstances should change.

Getting Paid

Fees are important, but no discussion of birds in the bush would be complete without birds in the hand. Indeed, it might be said that a VA has three primary tasks: finding clients, delivering excellent work, and getting paid. We're oversimplifying somewhat, but remove any one of these three components and the business will perish.

In this section, we'll focus on the third task—getting paid—and show you some simple methods to help assure that you're compensated for your work.

Fortunately, non-payment by clients isn't common in the VA industry, and many times the collection problem could have been avoided with a few protective measures up front. The following will help you stay on track for timely payments and avoid misunderstandings or "drive-offs":

1. Get it in writing!
2. Advance payments.
3. Retainers.
4. Invoices.
5. Follow up.
6. Accept credit card payments.

Get it in Writing!

If you've ever "channel surfed" on your TV, you've probably seen snippets of various court-related shows. If you lingered for even a minute, you likely heard the judge asking someone, "Did you get the agreement in writing?" We all know the reasoning behind that question: Written contracts are much easier to enforce.

Yet many new VAs, either out of carelessness or because they're uncomfortable asking the client to sign a contract, begin work on the basis of an oral agreement alone. But preparing and signing an agreement doesn't have to be a complex or stressful process. In fact, most clients will only respect you the more for your professional approach, and you can find contract templates easily on the Internet by using simple keyword search phrases such as the following:

✦ Template "independent contractor agreement."

✦ Sample "independent contractor agreement."

✦ "Sample contract" freelance.

✦ "Freelancing contract."

Though as we said before, we aren't attorneys and can't give legal advice, you will want to include in your template basic details such as:

+ The names of both parties.
+ A description of the services to be rendered.
+ The term of the agreement (start date and expiration date).
+ The payment amount and terms.
+ Confidentiality terms.
+ Provisions on the ownership of materials/information.
+ Warranties.
+ Indemnity terms.
+ A description of the relationship (clarifying that you are not an employee, but a contractor).

Speaking of lawyers, as you do your research, take some time to visit the sites of smaller law firms and solo practitioners, as well as other sites catering to small businesses and micro-enterprise. The Net abounds with free legal advice on many of the routine issues that small businesses face, and questions involving service contracts, independent contractors, and similar areas have already been answered by practicing attorneys hundreds, if not thousands of times. And if your situation varies from the norm, or just for reassurance's sake, you can always arrange a low-cost or free initial consultation with an attorney online or in your local community.

Advance Payments

Many VAs who work with clients on an as-needed or project basis require a portion of their payment up front. Most clients will be amenable to this arrangement, and those who aren't should be approached with a bit more caution.

A common method used in calculating an appropriate advance is 50 percent of the projected time cost, plus any materials the VA will need to complete the project. For example, if the VA quotes a price of $500 for his services, and $75 for supplies and materials, the client would be billed in advance for $325 (50 percent of 500 + 75). On completion of the project, the client is billed the remainder.

Remember of course that from the client's viewpoint, his funds are at risk until the project is done. Further, VAs supply services rather than tangibles, which means the client can't get in his car and drive by the construction site to see how his new house is doing. He has nothing to reassure him until the finished "product" is in hand. The remedy? Keep your client regularly updated on the status of the project, and be sure to include any news that the project might cost more than you anticipated. When glitches arise in a project, an informed client is likely to collaborate with you to find a mutually agreeable outcome, but a client who feels he's been deceived may leave you stuck with an unpaid bill.

Retainers

It's common practice for VAs to work with clients on a retainer basis. In these arrangements, the client typically purchases a "block" of time up front each month, assuring her that the VA will be available for a set number of hours and helping her manage her budget. The benefits to the VA are obvious as well, and many offer a reduced hourly rate to their retainer clients.

How do you estimate and apply the retainer? Typically, the VA and the client work together to ballpark the average number of hours needed per month, and the client pays in advance for those hours. (Of course, a retainer period may exceed a month, but a month is typical.) A separate bill is issued at the end of each period for any overages or material reimbursements.

Where retainers are used, be sure to inform your clients in timely fashion as they near the end of their pre-paid hours, so they can advise you how to proceed. In some cases, the client may tell you to forge ahead, but where budgets are limited they may ask you to stop when the retainer has run out. Naturally, this should always be the client's call.

Invoices

Invoices should always be sent out in a timely manner. Be sure that each includes the date, payment terms (payable on receipt, Net 30, and so forth), and a detailed accounting of services rendered. Some VAs have found that payment comes faster when they offer a discount for prompt payments.

If you opt to invoice clients after work is completed rather than billing in advance or working on retainer, be sure to invoice new clients weekly rather than bi-weekly or monthly. This will limit your exposure as you get to know the client and her payment habits.

Follow Up

If you don't receive payment by the due date, you should follow up promptly. Usually, a phone call or e-mail will do the trick, but you may need to send a duplicate invoice marked "past due." If a client is non-responsive or evasive, include a copy of your contract with the duplicate invoice. This subtle reminder that the client agreed in writing to pay you for your services will usually do the trick.

Accept Credit Card Payments

Letting your clients pay by credit card can dramatically reduce the time from invoice to payment. Obviously this can be a plus, especially in times of high inflation, when the "float" can eat into your profits.

Not so long ago, if a VA wanted to accept credit cards, she had to obtain a merchant account, a time-consuming and expensive process with set-up fees, processing fees, and usually some "miscellaneous" fees as well. (Most VAs didn't.) Now, largely thanks to eBay and similar sites, many low-cost methods of transferring funds have evolved, and companies such as PayPal (*www.paypal.com*), iBill (*www.ibill.com*), and WorldPay (*www.worldpay.com*) allow VAs to accept credit card payments without the time and expense associated with merchant accounts.

Of course, be sure to do your homework before signing up with any funds transfer agent. Compare their fees (most take about 3 percent of payments received on your behalf), any set-up charges, and their policies—particularly those affecting how and when funds will be transferred to your bank account.

CHAPTER 6

Setting Up Your Business and Your Office

You probably didn't think you could launch your "little home business" without a few government agencies weighing in and the law and tax folks having their say, and of course you're right. So in this chapter we'll cover some of the legal, tax, and regulatory issues that often arise, as we hearken to our lawyer's elbow in our side, and add, "Your mileage may vary!" (In other words, we aren't attorneys, accountants, financial advisors, or insurance agents, and we always recommend that new VAs consult an appropriate expert with any questions regarding their own unique circumstances.)

Naming Your Business

Co-author Chris Durst remembers toiling for days back in 1995 over what to name her VA practice. Her son Zachary, then 8, was the one who finally came up with the name that stuck. Zach had been listening to Chris bounce dozens of names around, and finally he said, "Hey, call it 'my staff,' Mom." When Chris asked him how he had thought of the idea, he replied, "Well, that way your clients can tell people, 'I'll have my staff take care of that,' and they won't be lying!" (Besides getting a good name for her business—My Staff, LLC—Chris gained some interesting insights into the inner workings of her son's mind. "The former was valuable," she says, "but the latter has been priceless—especially now that he's a teenager!")

The process of naming your business offers a great opportunity to let your creativity and wit shine through. (Don't let it bother you that the more obvious of the good names have probably already been taken—it's still great fun!) Here are a few thoughts to help make the business naming process entertaining but effective, too:

+ Keep your image and services in mind.
+ Get input from creative friends and family.
+ Remember that there's no name like your name.
+ Consider Website (domain name) availability.

Keep Your Image and Services in Mind

Think about the image you want to project as a VA, and make sure your company name conveys or reinforces it. For example, "Crazy Carla's" might work for a discount furniture store, but would you entrust your bookkeeping to "Crazy Carla"? Maybe "Capable Carla's Virtual Assistance Solutions" or "Carla's Competent Office Solutions" would better serve the purpose.

Though they may not have a lot of va-va-voom, words such as *superior, quality,* and *complete* can trigger positive reactions in the client's thinking. If possible, weave these types of words into the business name or tag line or, at the very least, avoid using words that leave negative impressions when used to describe professional services—such as *discount, cheap,* or *bargain.*

Of course, you should also have a look at the names other VAs are using. You'll probably find some you wish you had thought of first and others that leave you wondering what the VA was thinking! Analyze your reactions to various types of names. Do you notice any patterns in your preferences? Do you favor names that are sophisticated? Witty? To the point?

Though obviously you can't use a name that's already been taken, this process can give you a better sense of what appeals to you and what will appeal to the types of clients you want to work with. (And while you're at it, consider how the names you like will translate into Web addresses, which we'll touch on again shortly. Is it short? Memorable? Appropriate?)

Get Input From Creative Friends and Family

Their suggestions can sometimes seem wacky, but brainstorming with friends and family can often yield a strong business name. (It also sidesteps the blinders we occasionally wear when we're trying to name something so close to us. Ever wonder how some kids end up with goofy names? A little discussion might have helped!) And at the very least, it will stimulate your creative juices, which always come in handy at the launch of a business.

Remember That There's No Name Like Your Name

Don't get too attached to any business name until you can make sure it's not being used by another business. Trademark laws prohibit businesses from using the same name (or a name that is similar enough to cause confusion) as competing businesses, and, more to the point, you don't want to have to redo your Website, stationery, and all the rest of your marketing materials six months down the road when you get a "cease and desist" letter from an angry VA or other businessperson.

As an obvious first step, you can use your favorite search engine to hunt for your target name and close variations. (Don't forget to enter your names with and without quotes.) You should also check with your town hall, county clerk's office, and state corporation commission or Secretary of State to see if the name and near variants are registered there.

To sleep even better, you may also want to run searches at the U.S. Patent and Trademark Office Website (*www.uspto.gov*), which will cover registered businesses, and at the Thomas Register Website (*www.thomasregister.com*), which will include unregistered trademarks.

All this said, trademark law is complex, and attorneys' sites dealing with these and similar issues can give you the final word.

Consider Website (Domain Name) Availability

As you might guess, we strongly encourage every VA to have a Website—or at the very least reserve the business's domain name—as soon as he or she can afford it. Apart from all the marketing reasons, it'd be a shame to set up your business with the perfect name only to discover it had been taken.

This part of the name-clearing process is easy. Just go to the Network Solutions site (*www.networksolutions.com*) and click on the "whois" link, or to BetterWhois.com, Inc. (*www.betterwhois.com*), and type in your target domain name

(Web address). Consider variations for the best fit. For example, if your preferred business name was "ABC Virtual Assistance," you'd probably want to check the availability of both *"abc-virtualassistance.com"* and *"abcva.com."*

Registering Your Business Name

Any business name other than your personal name (that is, Mary Smith, Virtual Assistant) is usually deemed a trade or "fictitious" name, and may have to be registered under state or local laws. The process is usually simple—the clerk performs a database search, you submit a registration form, and you pay a fee (usually less than $50)—though in some states you'll also have to publish the proposed name in the local paper and show proof of publication. Registration helps protect the name from being used by someone else but brings other benefits, too, because many banks won't open a business account without it, and, if disputes arise, courts like to see registration as official evidence that your business exists.

In many states, fictitious business names are registered at the county level, but in others they're handled through the office of the Secretary of State. A call to your county clerk's office should put you on the right track for the procedures for your location.

Registering Your Business Name as a Trademark

Because of the time and expense, VAs and similar microenterprises rarely go to the trouble of registering their business names as trademarks. However—though it may vary by state—business names generally automatically receive what is called "common law" protection when the owner uses the name in commercial and brand-building activities. Placing the letters "TM" next to your business name, though not required, will show others that you're serious about protecting your name. (If you have any questions, or feel that your own situation is atypical, you should speak with a lawyer, as trademark law is far more complex than our brief summary here might make it seem.)

If you do decide to register your business name as a trademark, the process (in the United States) is handled through the federal Patent and Trademark Office (*www.uspto.gov*) and costs approximately $300.

Forms of Business Ownership

Now that you have a name for your business, you'll need to select the type of ownership structure that works best for you. Because this will also determine how your business is treated legally and how you and your business pay taxes, you'll want to choose carefully, and you may want to consult an attorney and accountant as well.

There are three basic legal forms of small-business ownership: sole proprietorship, partnership, and corporation. There's also a hybrid between a corporation and partnership, known as the limited liability company, or "LLC," which has become very popular in recent years. We'll give snapshots of these ownership types here, but again, you may want to consult specialists for the ramifications of each—or at the very least do additional research on your own—to see which form is optimal for your situation.

Sole Proprietorship

The sole proprietorship is the form that most closely identifies the business with the individual. (As you'll see, this can be good and bad.) Because of its simplicity and convenience, and because VAs usually work alone, the sole proprietorship is the most common form of business structure in the industry. As with other forms, it has benefits and disadvantages. We'll list the major ones here.

Advantages of a sole proprietorship

✮ Ease of organization: You simply register your business with the appropriate authorities.

✮ The individual has full control of the business (no shareholders, no board of directors), which enhances focus and streamlines decision-making and implementation.

✮ Income from the business belongs to the owner, and all cash flow goes to his or her personal tax return.

✮ Dissolution is simple: The owner may simply stop doing business.

Disadvantages of a sole proprietorship

✮ The owner has unlimited personal liability, legally and financially, for the activities of the business.

✮ Perception of smallness and instability. (Some clients may be more reassured seeing "Inc." or "LLC" beside the business name.)

✮ Harder to secure capital for the business.

Partnership

In this type of legal structure (uncommon in the VA industry, at least at present), two or more people share ownership of the business and may share control as well. To minimize the potential for misunderstandings and to provide mechanisms to settle disputes, partnership agreements are often prepared or reviewed by an attorney. Agreements also cover the sharing of profits and losses, how partners are admitted or dropped, and the partnership's dissolution. (We won't go into detail here, but partnerships also differ according to whether they are *general* or *limited*.)

Advantages of a partnership

✯ Easy to form (once the terms of the agreement are set).

✯ Separate legal entity.

✯ Management responsibilities can be shared.

✯ Partners can pool complementary skills.

✯ Profits go directly to the partner's personal income.

Disadvantages of a partnership

✯ General partners have unlimited liability for business obligations.

✯ Profits must be shared.

✯ Profits are taxed as personal income.

✯ Shared ownership may entail loss of focus, slower decision-making and implementation.

Corporation

As partnerships are, corporations—which may be either of two types, "C" or "S"— are separate legal entities, existing apart from the individuals who form or own them. One reason for their popularity is that their officers and shareholders are broadly shielded from personal liability for the entity's activities.

A C corporation may have an unlimited number of owners (shareholders), who may be individuals or other legal entities. Though corporate officers may sometimes be required to guarantee bank loans or notes with their own assets, personal liability is generally much more limited than is the case with other business structures.

Advantages of a C corporation

✯ Limited personal liability.

✯ Separate legal entity.

✯ Perpetual existence: It can survive death of "members" (shareholders).

✯ Ownership is easily transferred (sale of stock).

Disadvantages of a C corporation

✯ More regulated than other entities.

✯ Can be expensive to organize.

✯ Greater record-keeping obligations.

✯ "Double taxation" issues—both corporate and personal income is taxed.

The S (or Subchapter S, named for a subchapter of the Internal Revenue Code) corporation is very similar to the C corporation, but it elects to be taxed as a partnership. This means the corporation itself does not pay tax, but its income is taxable to the shareholders as personal income. Usually the S route is taken by corporations expecting operating losses, which can be passed straight to the shareholders for tax benefits.

The advantages and disadvantages of the S generally track those of the C corporation, except that the S avoids the double taxation of profits.

Limited Liability Company (LLC)

A limited liability company is a cross between a partnership and a corporation, offering owners the tax advantages of the first with the limited exposure of the second. The LLC is the second most popular business type among VAs.

Advantages of an LLC

✯ Taxed as an S corporation or a partnership is, avoiding double taxation of profits.

✯ Fewer restrictions than corporations.

✯ Limited liability for owners.

✯ Liquidation of the LLC is generally a tax-free event.

Disadvantages of an LLC

✯ More expensive to create than a sole proprietorship or simple partnership.

✯ State law may limit the life of an LLC.

✯ Must have at least two partners to obtain federal recognition.

✯ Earnings are generally subject to self-employment tax.

Permits and Licenses

You'll need to contact your local government to determine the licenses and permits required for your VA practice. Most locations will let you operate with minimal paperwork and expense, because VA businesses are "low-impact": no signage, no increase in foot or vehicle traffic, no discernible changes to the dwelling or neighborhood. Specialized or occupational permits are also usually waived, as VAs don't work with hazardous materials, food, children, medicine, or in other high-regulation categories.

It's possible that your county or city will require you to purchase a general "home occupation permit" for the business (application form, small fee) but most states reserve this for "regulated services" such as doctors, lawyers, realtors, and so forth. To be sure, check with your town, city, or county clerk's office and ask them what they recommend.

While we're on the subject of permissions, if you're renting an apartment you'll of course want to check your lease and touch base with the rental office to make sure you are "in bounds" with the landlord. The last thing you need is an eviction notice after months of effort and expense building your business.

Tax Registrations
Federal Requirements

Because the majority of VAs operate as sole proprietors, without employees, they don't have to apply for an Employer Identification Number (EIN). (Sole proprietors use their own social security number rather than an EIN.) Other business types, however, will require an EIN, which is usually obtained by filing IRS Form SS-4 (available at *www.irs.gov*).

State Tax Permits

Every business that sells *taxable* goods or services must obtain a sales tax license from the state in which it does business, so call your state revenue department to determine whether the services you plan to provide are taxable. (In many states, they won't be, particularly if your clients reside outside your state.)

This said, the Internet has introduced tax issues that still haven't been resolved (Congress, for example, is still debating the question of taxes on goods and services sold over the Internet) and, even if this weren't the case, tax rules and regulations are notorious for changing from year to year, and "small" details in an individual's situation can sometimes dramatically alter his or her tax picture. At the very least, as a responsible business owner, you'll want to keep up to date on tax issues through periodic visits to your state's Website and to the IRS site (*www.irs.gov*) as well. Sign up for e-mailed tax updates, read them, and touch base regularly with your book-keeper or accountant.

Insurance
Home Business and Auto Insurance

A recent study from the Independent Insurance Agents & Brokers of America (IIABA; *www.independentagent.com*) shows that the majority of home-based businesses are "vulnerable to significant financial losses because they do not have the proper business insurance coverage." The report goes on to say that, when questioned about the absence of insurance, 40 percent of respondents thought their business was covered by some other kind of insurance (such as their homeowner's policy), and 30 percent felt their business was "too small" to insure.

Home business owners who believe their homeowner's insurance also protects their businesses discover the truth when accidental damage or a theft hurts the business and they file a claim. Then they learn that a typical homeowner's policy won't cover the replacement cost of the computer system and other hardware, loss of business data, paper supplies, and other business-related inventory and equipment.

Home business owners often forgo adequate insurance because they fear high premiums. However, many insurance providers now offer "riders" for homeowner's policies that extend coverage to include the home-based business, and a separate and comprehensive commercial policy can cost as little as $250 a year. Because VAs usually don't have clients visiting the premises, personal injury liability is limited, which can lower premiums even further.

If your business grows to where you have employees working in your home, you'll need more substantial insurance coverage, including worker's compensation and increased personal injury liability. Touching base periodically with your insurance agent will assure that your policies match your needs. (Don't let yourself be oversold, of course. As with any professional, listen carefully to the recommendations, check out his or her suggestions with research of your own, and make the choice that's best for you.)

While you're talking to your agent, be sure to ask if your automobile insurance will cover the business use of your vehicle. VAs seldom use their automobiles primarily for their practice, so few changes, if any, may be required. Again, be candid about your situation, ask questions, and do what's best for you and your business.

Professional Liability Insurance

The need for professional liability insurance—also known as errors and omissions insurance—will vary among VAs, depending on the services they offer and the kinds of clients they represent. It's intended to cover the monetary damage a client suffers for faulty goods or service.

A good example might be a VA who specializes in event planning. The client has asked the VA to set up the company's annual corporate awards banquet for January 17th. The VA hires the band, reserves the ballroom, hires the caterer, and gets all the bells and whistles in line, but by mistake schedules everything for January 7th. A lot of the client's money has been spent for nothing and little, if any, is refundable. At times such as this, the VA needs professional liability coverage (or very deep pockets).

VAs who plan to work with attorneys, insurance brokers or agents, doctors, and financial advisors and in other high-end specialties will also want to discuss this type of insurance with their agent. We'd also recommend that they network with other VAs already experienced in these areas to see what kind of coverage and liability limits they've found most suitable. As with so many aspects of business and professional life, you can never be too knowledgeable.

Setting Up the Home Office

It may sound trivial, but make no mistake: Your work-place will definitely impact the course of your practice. Within the budget you've set, and regardless of whether you're just setting up a home office or assessing an existing workspace, there are three things to keep in mind: efficiency, profession-alism, and comfort.

Defining Your Work Area

Your home office should allow you to perform all neces-sary duties without unduly disrupting the rest of the house-hold and at a reasonable cost.

Many VAs find it helpful to separate their office some-what from the "personal" areas of the home. This shows the rest of the family that you're serious about your business and helps you assume and maintain a professional mindset. The space should of course be quiet, far or easily isolated from the sounds of children, pets, and household appliances.

If clients will come to call, your work area should require as little exposure as possible to the personal areas of the house. If feasible, a separate entrance (or even a detached building on your property) might be best.

Watch the Cost!

When we're designing or renovating a room of any kind, it's always tempting to go a little overboard, and where workspace is involved the rationalizations seem to come even easier. ("I'm going to be working my rear end off in here, so I deserve it!") But we'd encourage you to be on guard against this kind of thinking. Partitioning walls, installing wood paneling, soundproofing the ceiling, and laying down new carpeting can all be justified at some point, but the question is *when?* (Remember what we said about bootstrapping?) Keep initial spending on physical surroundings to the minimum, and allocate your startup budget wisely. (Up-to-date technology, for example, will feed your bottom line better than carpeting or fresh paint.) Later on, when the business is tractoring ahead, you can "reward" yourself with the upgrades you've always merited!

2-Second Spotlight

Saving on Client Credit Card Charges

Name: Natalie Wimberley

Business: Wimberley Business Solutions

URL: "I haven't needed one yet!"

Personal: Natalie Wimberley, an Air Force spouse and mother of one, completed Staffcentrix VA training and launched her business in Oklahoma in 2003. She specializes in real-estate assistance and database management.

I found a great money and time saver for accepting credit card payments. Previously, I was using an online service that charged a percentage of each transaction. I was spending approximately $70 a month in fees, and it was taking three to five business days for the funds to be transferred to my bank account. Then I discovered that my bank will allow my clients to call in and make a credit card "payment" to the bank. The bank then credits my account and the funds are available to me at the close of business the same day. There is no charge to me or my clients, and all I need to give out are my name and an ID number.

• • • • •

Equipping Your Home Office

As we've suggested, VAs should have the "right" equipment when they launch, but again, don't go overboard. Yes, it's gratifying to have an office with "all the bells and whistles," and surely we all deserve one, but start with the basics and add the rest as your budget allows. Look at equipment purchases as investments of valuable capital, to be made only after a careful analysis of the practice's needs.

We've included some items and discussion here to help you decide what's essential and what can wait. (If you plan to offer specialized services, you'll need to add items to match your needs.)

Furniture

The two most important pieces of furniture for your home office will be a large desk and a comfortable chair.

VAs often find themselves multitasking, so having plenty of desktop to spread out on will help you keep your projects separate. If you don't have a large desk already, consider buying used. You'll not only save money, but you may reap better quality too—solid wood rather than particleboard, metal instead of plastic. (Older desks are often bigger as well, made in the pre-Dilbert era when offices measured more than 20 square feet.)

Another option for the serious bootstrapper (who doesn't expect visits from clients) is to buy an interior door at the local lumberyard or Home Depot and bridge it between a pair of two-drawer filing cabinets. This will yield plenty of surface area and filing space too.

Workplace ergonomics is a perennial hot issue, and studies have shown repeatedly that a good chair is the most important factor in comfort and productivity. Test-sit as many types of chairs as you possibly can—you'll be spending many long hours in it—and look for one that doesn't dig into your thighs, make you feel like you're tipping overboard forward or backward, or have arms like an alien.

As with the desk, opt for used if needs dictate. Pampered executives frequently exchange perfectly good chairs for something in a new color or style. If you can't afford to upgrade your present chair, make do with a small pillow for your back and a footstool for your feet. When the business is cranking, you can order a throne!

Computer and Software

The tech marketplace changes too rapidly for us to make specific recommendations here, but we can say that, because VAs have such computer-reliant businesses, you should purchase the best computer you can afford. If your budget permits, include up-to-date hardware, with a large RAM, the fastest modem possible, a CD-ROM drive, a sound card, and, above all, a good monitor. (Your faithful eyes will thank you.)

Again, be careful not to overbuy. Yes, good systems are important, but they also become obsolete almost as quickly as you can unpack them. Buy something that will keep you humming for two or three years but that you won't still be paying down when it's time to upgrade.

Regarding software, be sure to consider your present *and future* client base. To use a basic example (you specialists know who you are), there are many word-processing applications around but, because most businesses use Microsoft Word or Word Perfect, it follows that these are "safe" purchases, compatible with the majority of your clients.

Don't forget to purchase a good anti-virus program—and urge your clients to use them too. The most common are Norton and McAfee, but others are available and continually emerging, so do your homework to see which suits best. (Apart from other features, we prefer those that update automatically online.)

Telephone System

Your phone system needn't be complex, but it must be dependable. Have at least two phone lines installed, if budget permits—one for phone, one for fax. (If you connect to the Net by dial-up, a third line is optimal, but your modem can share your fax line if necessary.)

A headset will help keep you productive (hands-free) and save you from "phone neck," too. Buy a cordless, if you can.

Long-Distance Provider

Although cost is important, don't discount the *quality* and *reliability* of a provider's services. A great rate won't do you much good if your calls don't go through, the lines are garbled, or you can't get prompt customer service when things go wrong.

Before you choose a long-distance company, see how you're treated when you first call up. Was the salesperson courteous? Was he or she interested in your business? Did he or she take the time to make sure you understood the details of the company's plans? Were you put on hold for an inordinate time?

Chances are that if the company's service wasn't very good initially, it won't be much better after you've signed on.

When considering your long-distance options, be sure to find out if the carrier has an "account coding" feature. With this, you can assign each of your client accounts a code (usually two or three digits), so that when you place a call on their behalf it will be billed to that account. (You'll still get the invoice from your phone company, but the calls will be separated and totaled by account.) This feature will save you a *tremendous* amount of time, because you won't have to log outgoing calls and do a line-by-line dissection of your phone bill each month.

Answering Machine or Voice Mail

Few things are more irritating to time-starved businesspeople than trying repeatedly to reach someone by phone and getting a busy signal or no answer. Answering machines are entry-level options, but go for voice mail through your phone company if you possibly can. It will usually sound more professional, and your messages won't be lost or unrecorded in the event of a storm or technical glitch.

Facsimile Machine

VAs communicate predominantly through e-mail and file attachments, so a mid-priced fax machine will often suffice. But you'll definitely need a stand-alone fax. Computer-based faxing programs are great for receiving documents and sending information you've stored in your system, but they don't do paper!

Down the Road

As your practice grows, you'll have a clear idea of what you need and what you can live without. We preach frugality, but nevertheless, don't let yourself be penny-wise and client-poor. A thriving practice may well need a faster modem or broadband access, a scanner, a magnetic tape backup, an emergency power backup, or all of the above! The key thing to remember at all points of the business is to keep capacity and profits in sync.

CHAPTER 7

Building a Healthy Foundation for Your Business

With the nuts and bolts of setting up your business behind you, let's turn to how you'll build a healthy foundation of work and clients that will support your practice in the coming years.

At the center of a healthy VA practice are carefully selected clients for whom the VA provides excellent service doing work she or he loves. Put another way—and this is true of most if not all service industries—the type of clients you choose, and your relationship with them, will greatly define your working life.

In a moment we'll speak of our philosophy of how successful VAs "partner" with their clients. But first, let's put the horse back in front of the cart and spend some time on the importance of choosing your clients wisely.

The Client Makes the Practice

We accept it as obvious that, in any close relationship, the identity of the other party is paramount. Yet day after day, people choose their working relationships—which in many ways are at least as significant to us as emotional relationships and involve far more of our waking life—with scarcely more thought than they would give to where they buy their clothes. And then they wonder why they are unhappy with their jobs!

How many times has a job that you would otherwise have enjoyed been spoiled by the personality of a boss or supervisor or the quirks or abrasiveness of clients or customers? Yet we grit our teeth and keep getting up and driving back into work, for the security (such as it may be) of the job and the paycheck. One of the greatest rewards of being a VA is being free to choose exactly who you'll be working with—your own "significant working others."

We'll say it again: The character of your clients will directly determine the tenor, pace, and "emotional payoff" of your practice. Silk purses don't come from sows' ears. The client makes the practice!

Defining Your Ideal Client

Though every VA will define his or her ideal client differently, desirable clients share certain core qualities. The attractive VA client:

✦ Wants a professional-to-professional relationship—a partnership—with you.

✦ Understands the value of your services.

✦ Pays your fee at the agreed-upon rate and on time.

✦ Values your input in matters involving your areas of expertise.

✦ Communicates his needs and wishes clearly and comprehensively.

✦ Takes responsibility for her role in achieving her goals.

✦ Doesn't need to be "right" all the time.

As you create a profile of your ideal client, be sure to consider your own personality and how you interact or "click" (or don't) with different types of people. For example:

✦ Are you more of a refined, gentle, or thoughtful type, who will have trouble partnering with a rough-hewn, louder, shoot-from-the-hip personality?

✦ Do you prefer working relationships that are more casual ("Hi, Fred"), or more formal ("Good afternoon, Mr. Hollingsworth")?

✦ Are you a "color outside of the lines" (creative) type who finds it difficult to work with "paint by numbers" (linear) personalities?

Don't waste your chance to avoid the kinds of people who have been ruining your day. Spend time on your list. Do "nit-pickers" and "anal-retentives" drive you nuts? Show 'em the door. Don't like micro-managers? Hit the "delete" button. Whiners and "needy" people get you down? Off with their heads! Don't be shy or reluctant—this is strictly between you and you!

The Art of Miscalculation

Prospective client you don't care for

+ Work you don't like

A chance to make money

New VAs make this miscalculation often, and it skews the development of their practice. How does this happen? Through the phenomenon of "like follows like." Let's say you've decided you'll never work with lawyers—you don't like the personality types, and the work bores you. The prospective client is a lawyer. You accept him, and he loves your work. Who is he going to refer you to? "Like follows like"—other lawyers! A year later, your client list is 90 percent lawyers and legal work, and you hate your life!

New VAs can fall into this trap for many reasons, most often because:

✦ Their spouse or significant other is saying, "Show me the money!"

✦ They don't understand the dynamics of practice development—how "like follows like."

✦ The client seems desperate for help and they feel guilty about turning him away.

Whatever the reason, and no matter how strong the temptation, try to resist giving in and adding a "bad brick" to your foundation. You will thank yourself later on!

Interviewing Prospective Clients

As in most other work-related interviews, VA-client interviews are "two-way streets": The interviewing is mutual. Here, however, mutuality weighs even more heavily because of the partnership factor. Above all, go into the interview armed with a detailed list of what you need to know about the prospect. (We'll give you some thought-starters.) And be sure to *keep your antennae up*! This will probably be a phone interview with e-mail components and, until we all have real-time desktop video, you won't have facial signals and body language to read from. Turn your intuition to "high"!

20 Key Points to Consider in Exploring the Prospective Relationship

1. What are the client's chief reasons for seeking a VA? (High workflow? Lost an employee or temp?)

2. If workflow is high, what are the causes? Increased marketing or sales? Excessive layoffs?

3. If a key administrative assistant or other employee has left, why?

4. Similarly, check the client's general staffing picture. Has he or she had a number of VAs, employees or temps who "just haven't worked out"?

5. If so, will you be able to "work out"? Can this client be satisfied?

6. Ask the client to talk a bit about his or her niche or industry. How's competition? What's the outlook? Does the client seem well-informed? Sufficiently sophisticated?

7. Does the client sincerely want to partner? (For example, some prospects will know they need help, but can't delegate well. Others may be "too shy"—overly protective of information critical to the relationship, which may hobble it as time goes on. These potential trouble spots need to be uncovered in the interview.)

8. What are the client's overall expectations for the partnership?

9. Do these expectations seem reasonable? Measurable?

10. By what criteria will the client measure the success or failure of the partnership?

11. How does the client visualize the partnership helping him or her reach corporate goals?

12. Are the client's overall priorities clear—to him or her as well as to you?

13. Make sure that the role the client is describing for you doesn't run counter to his or her "business psychology" (or in a corporation's case, its "culture"). Otherwise, you'll be headed for conflict and possible failure as well. For example, is the client:

    ✦ Bottom line–driven?

    ✦ Growth-driven?

    ✦ Operations-oriented?

14. Does the client have any other partnerships or contractual relationships that could hamper or limit your ability to achieve your mutual objectives?

15. Who makes relevant decisions in the client's organization? (Who are you "really" answering to?)

16. Ask the client about working style. Highly organized? More "laid back"? Detail-oriented, or "just give me the gist"?

17. Get a feel for the client's work pace. Slow and steady? "Workaholic"? Can you keep pace without distorting your practice or unbalancing your family life?

18. Get a sense of how the client handles stress. Is he or she an "exploder"? A "simmerer"? Are you compatible? Go with your gut.

19. Be attuned to the client's decision-making processes. Scattered? Ad hoc? Linear?

20. Ask the client to describe their working strengths *and weaknesses.* (If they can't admit to any, think twice about the relationship!)

Remember that these questions are meant to be issue-prompters rather than a road map. Track the list too closely and you may scare the client off! Hone in on the issues that are the most important to you.

Finally, as you undertake and complete the "communication dance" with the prospective client:

✦ Be clear about your own expectations and preferences.

✦ Know what you're prepared to trade off and what you won't give up. Know your "deal-breakers" before the interview. This will help your concentration and give your intuition free rein.

✦ Don't rush the deal. These are weighty decisions. What's the motto? *Clients make the practice!* They are the "dog," not the "tail"!

Once you've decided to partner, you might consider as your first step working with the client at no charge to develop clear short- and long-term partnership goals. This assures that you're both using the same benchmarks, triggers the critical "gelling" process, and reduces the chances of significant disappointments and frustration later on.

And as in any other engagement, never be afraid to walk away if it doesn't feel right.

Partnering With Your Clients

Unlike the employee-employer relationship—which, despite the "team member" confectionery that many employers now use to coat it, often seems more akin to a "serf-landowner" relationship—the VA-client link is almost unavoidably a partnership: *an evolving, symbiotic professional (and often personal) bond, where the success and welfare of each is intertwined with that of the other.* And once you experience the difference, you'll wonder how you ever settled for serfdom.

Successful virtual partnerships are based on a mutual understanding that VA and client will vigorously and proportionately pursue agreed-upon goals. And just as you'll outline for your clients what you can do for them, you must tell them what you'll need *from* them for your role to be honored and fulfilled. This collaborative approach not only promotes effectiveness and high morale, but it reinforces the professional-to-professional mindset that keeps the relationship humming.

Depending on your practice and field, you might consider putting a page on your Website that lays out your philosophy on VA-client partnerships. (To our knowledge, co-author Chris can take credit for this innovative step in client-professional relations, which first appeared on her VA Website in 1995 and has been widely copied since.) This assures even casual prospects of your potential devotion to their cause and helps maintain the mutual understanding you've struck with ongoing clients.

Your statement should be collegial but concise. It might look something such as this:

Our Partnering Philosophy

Our clients take a uniquely effective approach to "getting the job done" by partnering with us. In turn, we take quite seriously our commitment to them to produce optimal results.

Our relationship with our clients is a genuine partnership—a dynamic extension of their organization and ours. Focused, synergistic, and highly productive, our efforts blend to achieve mutual goals with maximum effectiveness. We are committed to developing long-term relationships with our clients that unfailingly achieve their objectives.

A review of our site will provide highlights of our notable efforts on behalf of our clients. However, a successful partnership requires commitment by both parties. Here are some key attributes we look for in our clients, to assure we are both on the road to a successful relationship. Our ideal client:

* Can clearly define his/her goals as well as time and money constraints;

* Clearly communicates his/her expectations and requirements;

* Is not sparing of information that is necessary to complete the project;

* Is available to answer questions or take comments;

* Helps meet deadlines;

* Expresses criticisms and concerns promptly and openly;

* Gives timely feedback;

* Respects and values our expertise; and

* Actively contributes to our efforts to achieve client goals.

Through this joint commitment, we forge partnerships that accelerate your business growth and give you the highest return on your investment.

● ● ● ● ●

Preparing for Effective Communications in Virtual Partnerships

Research indicates that 75 percent of what a person "really means" is communicated nonverbally—a statistic that shouldn't be taken lightly as you prepare to step into an industry where face-to-face collaboration is the exception rather than the rule.

Think for a moment about the way people communicate in traditional work environments. Nuances in facial expressions, hand gestures, the distance between the speakers, choice of venue ("Can you step into my office for a minute and shut the door?"), eye contact—all of these and much more tell us "what's up."

Consider, too, how assignments are communicated in physical space. Often, work is delegated and received through a "let me show you how" technique in which the person doing the assigning physically demonstrates what he or she wants the other person to do.

However, until real-time videoconferencing becomes common (and even this, of course, is just a shadow of the physical experience), all of these mechanisms and subtleties will remain lost to most VAs and their clients. This means that both parties must develop their communication skills *beyond what is normally thought superior, especially where listening is concerned.* If you can work on those skills now, as you ramp up your business, you'll not only wow your prospects in the interviews, you'll partner with them more effectively when you've added them to your roster.

In our training classes, we have aspiring VAs participate in an exercise where they pair up on a project and give and receive detailed instructions without looking at each other. This helps them understand the difficulties and frustrations that can sometimes arise between VA and client. We encourage you to recruit a friend or family member and try this exercise yourself.

"No-See" Communications Exercise

To do this exercise, you'll need two identical building models. In class, we usually use simple Lego models. Their building sets designed for ages 6 to 16, with 20–40 pieces, are ideal for making the exercise informative without being overly frustrating and usually cost less than $4 each.

Before you begin, you and your partner will need to decide who will role-play the Virtual Assistant and who will role-play the client. When you've chosen, the client should take both models and, out of sight of the VA, open one, remove the instructions, and give the pieces to the VA. The client keeps the boxes that the models came in, the pieces to one model, *and* the instructions, and may use them all to accomplish his or her goal.

Seat yourselves back-to-back, with each of you facing a table or flat work surface. It's now the job of the client, using spoken words alone, to guide the VA through the process of building the model. The VA may not look at what the client is doing, nor may the client observe the VA's work until her project is complete and ready to deliver to the client.

This simple exercise can be very revealing, and although "model-building" may not be on the list of services you expect to offer as a VA, the lessons you learn can help you communicate more effectively in your business relations as well as in your personal life.

We don't usually share this part of the training exercise but, if you and your partner have someone else watching the exercise, they're likely to find things pretty amusing (as you may, too). In our classes, where most people have never met before, seeing mature adults sitting with their backs to each other, staring down at models that they've just been told are designed for 6-year-olds, and watching as their faces begin to show determination, horror, puzzlement, or fits of the giggles— well, it's a lot of fun! We also see communication styles varying greatly—from silly to serious, linear to loony. But in the end, everyone manages to see the task through to completion, and the give-and-take has helped new friendships to blossom, too.

In every class, there is one partnership that breezes through the exercise with amazing ease. Without exception, these pairs share certain techniques and attitudes. Take a moment and think about how they may apply to the communications challenges you may encounter in your own practice:

✯ The client is committed to giving the best instructions she can.

✯ The VA asks questions freely if directions are unclear.

✯ The VA and client work together creatively to find a shared language, assigning names to different types of parts to simplify identification.

✯ The parties communicate flexibly and dynamically, both fully engaged in asking questions and offering suggestions to reach the goal.

Train Yourself to Listen

When it comes to effective virtual communications, a VA who listens well will always fare better than one who feels the need to do most of the talking. A client's "perception of reality" is his or her reality, and he or she will decide, act, and react based on this foundation. Listening well will not only help you hit your marks on any given project, but will furnish you a comprehensive picture of who your client is and where he or she wants to go. The result? Your effectiveness and value to your client increase dramatically.

Here are some tips to help you improve your listening skills and get the most out of every dialogue with your clients:

* Avoid multi-tasking. (It's tempting, but makes it harder to focus on the dialogue, and clients will sense your distraction, too.)

* Stay glued to what is actually being said; don't anticipate. (Trying to guess what's coming next usually means missing what's coming out.)

* Resist the impulse to interrupt. (It breaks the flow of the dialogue, may offend, and can take the client's thoughts off track.)

* Ask more questions and make fewer comments. (Questions show that you're "tracking" and open up the dialogue. Expanding the dialogue can also mean expanding opportunity.)

* Learn to "lubricate" conversations with comments such as "Yes, I see" and "I understand." These show you're listening, confer value on what's being said, and encourage further conversation.

* To minimize miscommunication, paraphrase the client's words. Example: "So what you're saying is..." or "If I'm understanding correctly, you'd like me to...." (Many VAs say this is one of their favorite techniques for clarifying assignments over the phone.)

* Make brief notes of key points for quick reference.

* Do your best to block outside interruptions.

Practicing these and other similar techniques will help you and your clients get the best out of every conversation.

Your Strengths, Weaknesses, and Target Market

In the next chapter, we'll explore in detail the most effective ways to market your practice and send a message to the marketplace that your prospects can't ignore. But first, you'll need to know a bit more about how you compare to other VAs, and how to identify—and master the language of—your target market.

The SWOT Analysis: Assessing Your Strengths and Weaknesses

Many companies use an exercise called a SWOT analysis to help determine the direction their business should take. It's designed to help you flesh out your Strengths and Weaknesses and examine the Opportunities and Threats your business may face. It brings into relief your abilities, assets, vulnerabilities, and competition, and it clarifies what you'll need to do to leverage advantages and surmount or avoid barriers to your success.

Each step of the SWOT should be approached systematically, and always with your end purpose—launching a successful and sustainable practice—in mind.

Start by creating a grid with four squares—two over two—and label the top two squares "Strengths" and "Weaknesses" and the lower two "Opportunities" and "Threats." Assess yourself and your situation in each of the four areas, and write your thoughts in the corresponding spaces. Following are some explanations and considerations that you might take into account as you work your way through the exercise.

Strengths (The Elements of Your Competitive Edge)

With maximum candor, list all the strengths that you and your projected business possess. Be realistic, and try not to let modesty or pride influence your judgment. Consider inviting others to join in—the input of neutral outsiders can be helpful—and brainstorm with them to find additional words or phrases that characterize your practice or professional profile. Write them down as people say them, and draw from these ideas to make your final "strengths" list.

Here are some points to consider as you analyze your strengths:

✲ What are your "advantages," your "superiorities"?

✲ What do you truly enjoy doing?

✲ What do you do well?

✲ Do you have a good personal or professional reputation?

✲ If you asked employers, coworkers, and others to name your strengths, what would they say?

✲ Don't forget that a supportive family, financial security, sound health, or other positive elements of your private life should also be listed.

✲ If you find this exercise difficult, try writing down a list of your "characteristics." (Some of these will hopefully be strengths!)

Weaknesses (The Areas Where the Competition Outperforms You)

List all the shortcomings or vulnerabilities you can think of that would apply to your personal and business profile. Include such things as knowledge and expertise, counterproductive habits such as procrastination or pessimism, weaknesses in equipment or finances, and so forth. Again, be honest. It's better to be frank now, and deal with any "unpleasant truths" early rather than late!

Points to consider as you analyze your weaknesses include:

✯ What could be improved?

✯ Where have you experienced occasional failures?

✯ What should be avoided (market sectors, types of services or prospective clients, business expansion scenarios that wouldn't work for you, and so forth)?

As with strengths, weaknesses should be considered from both personal and third-party viewpoints. Do other people perceive weaknesses that you might have missed? Do your competitors perform better in some areas than you yourself could?

Bear in mind that a strength can sometimes function as a weakness, too. For example, "perfectionism" is a strength insofar as it drives you to produce excellent results, but it's a weakness when it causes you to miss deadlines or lose your temper when someone or something "fails to measure up."

Opportunities (The Trends or Market Situations Ripe for Your Advantage)

When you look at your marketplace, what do you see? What are your competitors doing wrong? What needs are they failing to meet? Seek out gaps that you're qualified—and would like—to fill. (And keep in mind that some gaps may not last long! What you see as an opportunity today may soon be gone. Is the window wide enough for practical action?) This section of your SWOT is designed to help you map out your first "best" opportunities.

Here are some points to consider as you analyze your opportunities:

✯ Where are the good chances, the "ripe crops," in your marketplace?

✯ What interesting business trends are emerging in your region? Nationally? Internationally?

✯ Don't limit your thinking. Important opportunities may come from unlikely sources. For example, a company's downsizing can trigger the need for outsourced assistance while management adjusts to a smaller workforce.

✯ How might you make the most of your strengths or address your weaknesses to create additional opportunities?

Opportunities can also arise from:

✯ Technological developments (new software, new communications options, and so on).

✯ Changes in government policy related to your field.

✯ Changes in social patterns, population profiles, lifestyles, and so forth.

✯ Local events. (Remember: "Virtual" can also embrace "local.")

✯ Your status as a woman or member of a minority group, a veteran, a military spouse, and so on.

Threats (The Forces and Factors That Could Harm Your Practice)

List the factors that threaten the potential success of your business. What current or future trends might render your services less attractive, less useful, or obsolete? What are your competitors doing to outrun, mis-position, or outmaneuver you? What aspects of your personal life might hobble or endanger your business?

Points to consider as you analyze threats to your practice include:

✯ What obstacles (to launching, operations, growth) do you face?

✯ Are the standard specifications or requirements for your services or projects changing?

✯ Are changes in technology eroding your position (or improving others')?

✯ Do you have severe debt or cash-flow problems?

• • • • •

Once you've completed your analysis, it's time to review the information and formulate effective strategies. What you're aiming for is an "action plan" that *builds on strengths, resolves weaknesses, exploits opportunities,* and *avoids threats.* (If you can convert weaknesses and threats into strengths, and expand as well as exploit opportunities, the marketplace will give you a generous helping of extra credit!)

An action plan needn't assume a specific format, but should address questions such as the following:

✯ What steps will I take to capitalize on my immediate opportunities?

✯ What weaknesses can I improve upon to enter areas of significant opportunity?

✯ What specific measures can I take near-term to evade, neutralize, or repel hostile players or trends?

✯ Which weaknesses need to be addressed promptly?

✯ Which weaknesses should I simply respect now and address later?

The SWOT analysis you draft today is a "snapshot" of the current situation, but circumstances change and your action plan should change with them. It's wise to update your SWOT at least annually, so you don't overlook or get blindsided by new and significant developments.

Who Is "Your" Market?

Actor Bill Cosby, whose staying power as an entertainer and producer has impressed so many in the entertainment world, once said, "I don't know the key to success, but the key to failure is trying to please everybody."

There's a lot of wisdom in this quote, and VAs can learn from its message. Not every market is *your* market and, though it may run counter to your instincts, you can almost always build a healthier client base if you market to a smaller segment of the business population. This is called "niche marketing"— a strategy that involves highly-focused promotion to a smaller portion of a larger market—and we highly recommend it.

2-Second Spotlight

VAs and the Pet-Sitting Industry

Name: Becky O'Neil

Business: PetConnex, LLC

URL: *www.petconnex.com*

Personal: Becky O'Neil is the co-founder of PetConnex, LLC, a business development and consulting company specializing in the pet-sitting industry, and the president of Becky's Pet Care, Inc., which she launched from her home in 1998. Becky's Pet Care now has its own office space, 1,500 clients, 40 pet-sitters, and two full-time administrative assistants. Becky lives in Arlington, Virginia, with her son and daughter and her black Lab, Kate.

Professional pet-sitting is one of the fastest-growing home-based businesses in the world today. The benefits of owning a professional pet-sitting business include low start-up costs, the ability to manage the business from your home, and the chance for pet lovers to do something they enjoy. Many entrepreneurs starting a professional pet-sitting business have never owned a business before and have a limited scope of business knowledge and experience. My company, PetConnex, LLC, which consults to the pet-sitting industry, has been delighted to let these entrepreneurs know about the wonderful resources available to them through Virtual Assistants.

Pet-sitting business owners typically start their business on a small budget and initially do everything themselves—the pet care, the bookkeeping and accounting, the sales and marketing, the business development, answering the phone, scheduling, and on and on. VAs offer them a fabulous opportunity to have a professional team on hand to help with any task that they find cumbersome, overwhelming, or daunting—all at an affordable price!

Pet-sitting entrepreneurs can use Virtual Assistants to do their scheduling, reply to e-mails, answer the phone, do their invoicing and collections, pay the bills, maintain the books, maintain client correspondence, design their Website, develop a corporate identity and branding, design marketing materials, and manage public relations. Business owners can then spend their time and energy on the business tasks that they enjoy—and the pets in their care. They can leave the rest up to their dependable VA!

• • • • •

The Benefits of Niche Marketing

There's a story about a man who decides to take up hunting with a bow and arrow. He goes to the store and outfits himself with a quality bow, fine arrows, camouflage clothing—the works. He sets up a target in his backyard and practices faithfully until his every shot strikes the bull's-eye.

But in his eagerness to become a precise shooter, the man neglects to scout the woods to determine where the game is. He doesn't know where they gather, what they feed on, the paths they frequent, or where they rest. When hunting season finally opens, the man wanders into the woods and picks a random place to sit. As he shoots an arrow off into the woods, he says, "Ah! That's a perfect shot! I sure hope something walks into it!"

Many VAs, when they set about looking for clients, take the same approach as this hunter: The "whole world" is their target. They hone their expertise, plan every inch of their operations, grind out text for their Websites, and start shooting "marketing arrows" in every direction in hopes of "bagging a client." Unfortunately, this usually leads to wasted time, energy, and money; lots of frustration; and very few good clients.

Identifying your niche, or target audience, simplifies your marketing strategy, your planning and execution. By focusing exclusively on prospective clients in a single area or small group of specialties, you'll understand their needs and concerns in exceptional depth and can tailor your message clearly and effectively to the solutions they want most.

To illustrate how niche marketing streamlines the selling process, let's say you've worked in small accounting firms and very much enjoyed the experience. Accordingly, you've decided to target smaller firms and solo CPAs. Chances are, as in other professions, most of your prospects will be reading the same magazines, trade publications, newspapers, and e-zines; participating in the same e-mail lists (listservs) and message boards; and will belong to the same professional organizations and attend the same conferences. All of this makes it much easier for you to design and deliver an efficient and hard-hitting marketing campaign to your target audience.

Identifying Your Target Market(s)

In the next chapter, we'll explore the marketing process in much more detail, and you'll begin developing your own Strategic Marketing Plan—your marketing blueprint. For now, your focus should be on simply "getting the lay of the land," and narrowing down your possible targets.

2-Second Spotlight

VAs and the Financial Advisor Niche
Name: David J. Drucker, MBA, CFP
Business: Drucker Knowledge Systems
URL: *www.daviddrucker.com*

Personal: David J. Drucker, MBA, CFP is the co-author of *The Tools & Techniques of Practice Management*, released in December 2004 by The National Underwriter Company, and *The One Thing... You Need to Know from Each of the Industry's Most Influential Coaches, Consultants and Visionaries* (The Financial Advisor Literary Guild, 2005), which is available at *www.onethingforadvisors.com*, He is also co-author of *Virtual Office Tools for a High-Margin Practice: How Client-Centered Financial Advisors Can Cut Paperwork, Overhead, and Wasted Hours* (Bloomberg Press, 2002) and editor of the monthly newsletter *Virtual Office News (www.virtualofficenews.com)*.

Q: *How do you see the Virtual Office trend and virtual support needs of financial advisors developing over the next five years, and what Virtual Assistant services are in highest demand now?*

A: I believe the Virtual Office trend in the U.S. will achieve geometric growth over the next five years with continuing advances in associated technologies and social customs.

The adoption of e-mail—the workhorse of virtual communications—will approach 100 percent of the population at the same time as wireless Internet access becomes ubiquitous. The Internet, in turn, will continue to empower individuals to work independently while collaborating with others through the further development of online "meeting places" such as *www.intranets.com* and *www.webex.com,* as well as "bridge lines" for phone conferencing.

With these technologies becoming widespread, social custom will evolve past its sometimes acceptance of telecommuting to embrace all manner of remote work styles by employees and Virtual Work Partners (that is, outsourcing relationships).

As this evolution occurs, financial advisors will gradually adopt these new technologies and concomitant mindsets to preserve profit margins through the greater efficiency afforded by the virtual office. They will also demand more from their Virtual Assistants. VAs serving financial advisors will need to acquire specialized skills and knowledge, such as an understanding of the forms and procedures of financial custodians like Charles Schwab or TD Waterhouse so they can service the financial accounts of advisor clients—that is, open new accounts, transfer client funds between accounts, and set up automatic account distributions. VAs will also need to function as initial points of contact for sole practitioner advisors—taking client calls and directing them to the advisor or a Virtual Work Partner, handling client emergencies when advisors take much-needed vacations, and even screening calls from prospective clients.

The VA who serves more than a few financial advisors may even find him- or herself specializing in the needs of the financial advisor client to the exclusion of other types of small business clients.

• • • • •

Following is a small sampling of niche markets, many of which, of course, may be divided further into sub-categories (for example, corporate attorneys, tax attorneys, criminal defense attorneys, and so forth). When choosing your niche(s), don't limit yourself to one if there are several you feel you could excel in; you can always broaden or narrow the field as your business grows.

Sample Niche Markets

Attorneys	Authors
Professors	Building Contractors
Consultants	Business Coaches
Real Estate Agents	Architects
Doctors	Engineers
Churches/Synagogues/ Mosques	Public Relations Professionals
Accountants	Professional Speakers
Freelance Writers	Financial Investors
Entertainers	Entrepreneurs
Pet Services	Nonprofits
Physical Therapists	Professional Trainers
Individuals	Hair Salons
Associations	Insurance Brokers/Agents
Call Centers	Human Resource Managers
Import/Export Companies	Web Developers

● ● ● ● ●

Now, think of five niches you'd most like to concentrate on, and write them down. (This may seem as if it's a lot of targets, but you'll probably eliminate one or more in the next step of the selection process.) As you work up your list, consider the following questions:

+ Looking back at the jobs you've held, which was your favorite, and why?

+ Do you already have a network or good contacts in a given industry?

+ Of the services you've included in your "service menu," which would you most like to provide?

+ Do you have any interests or hobbies that could translate into niche markets? (For example, if you're an avid bicyclist, you might want to target bike shop owners, bicycling associations or groups, and/or writers who cover the sport.)

+ Do you work best with people of a certain age? Gender? Ethnicity?

+ If you could work in any industry, what would it be?

+ When people praise your work or some aspect of your personality, what do they mention most?

+ When you "daydream," what do you picture yourself doing?

Next, you'll "weigh" each of your niche choices to see how feasible they actually are. On a scale of one to 10, with 10 being the highest, score each niche in the eight areas listed on the following chart. (Note: N1 represents the first niche you've selected, N2 the second, and so on. If your list contains more than five, use a separate sheet of paper.)

Assessment Area	Niche/Score				
	N1	N2	N3	N4	N5
Sample: *I would be happy working* *in this niche on a daily basis.*	6	3	10	8	7
I would be happy working in this niche on a daily basis.					
I have the skills and knowledge to serve this niche well.					
I would like working with the types of people who work in this industry.					
The services and solutions I provide will appeal to this audience.					
This niche will want (not just need) what I have to offer.					
The people in this industry will understand the value of what I do.					
The prospects in this group have the money to pay for my services.					
I feel confident in my ability to create a unique marketing message that will compel this audience to buy my services.					
NICHE SCORES					

In the "niche scores" block at the bottom of each column, tally the score for each niche. Those with the highest scores will be the most promising for you, and you should give them serious consideration. If only one niche received a high score, don't worry; it could be that this is where your true calling lies, and you may never need (or wish) to pursue another. In your top choice(s), note where you have assigned low scores and work toward making improvements in those areas.

2-Second Spotlight

The Real Estate Industry as a Niche Market

Name: Michael J. Russer

Business: RUSSER Communications

URL: *www.russer.com*

Personal: Michael Russer is a highly acclaimed international speaker, author, and leading voice for the use of virtual outsourcing within the real estate industry and small business in general. He is also the cofounder of two Virtual Assistant organizations that serve the real estate industry.

The real estate industry is one of the most fertile sources of new business available for VAs wanting to specialize in helping REALTORS. First of all, it is a huge market with more than 2 million licensees in the United States alone. Also, any real estate salesperson who truly wants to succeed cannot possibly do everything that needs to get done alone. Having assistance is a prerequisite to having a satisfying and financially rewarding real estate sales career.

The entire scope of possible REALTOR assistance breaks down into two major categories: marketing support and operational support. Naturally, the typical "up and coming" sales associate will be primarily interested in boosting their business with marketing support, whereas the seasoned top producer will likely be much more interested in saving time through operational support. It is important to note here that, because of the vicissitudes of this commission-only industry, VAs may find more consistent and longer-term work supporting the more seasoned veteran salesperson.

Areas ripe for marketing support include "drip" e-mail campaign management, online lead management, pay-per-click search engine positioning, listing marketing coordination, direct mail campaigns, managing FSBO (for sale by owner) and expired listing campaigns, virtual tours, and keeping the agent's Website up to date. Bear in mind that if an agent asks you to have direct contact (via phone, e-mail, or regular mail) with any prospect or client, you will need to make sure those activities will not require that you have a license in the jurisdiction where the agent is located. Main areas of operational support include online transaction management, contact management (keeping the contact database up to date), classified and display ad management, CMA and listing presentation preparation, and screening e-mail and phone.

The real estate industry offers a tremendous opportunity for any VA who is hard working, diligent and can work effectively with high-strung sales-type personalities. And the best part is, you will never run out of potential clients!

• • • • •

Industry Immersion: Thinking as Your Audience Does

If you're already working as an employee or temp in your target niche, you won't need to be reminded of the value of immersing yourself in the culture of your target clients—you're already "swimming." However, if you've been out of the workforce for a while, or want to burrow into your target industry in more detail, then what follows should be right on point.

As with individual companies, industries too have cultures of their own, a way of thinking and speaking and looking at the world. Though it may take time to master, successful VAs know it's time well spent.

Because an industry's culture is distilled into its language— usually a mix of jargon and acronyms that only insiders understand—the better you speak the "tongue" of your niche markets, the more effective your marketing and communications generally will be. For example, if freelance writers are your target clients, you'll need to be at home with language such as, "Please send a tear sheet and a SASE along with that article, and include a note stating that I can change the slant if needed." (Translation: "Please send samples of my published work and a self-addressed stamped envelope along with that article, and include a note stating that I can change the story to address a certain readership if needed.")

To learn or stay current on your niche's culture—its news, trends, expert opinions, events—be sure to read its trade publications. As you do, consider how an article of your own might fit within their editorial needs, which we'll cover in more detail in the next chapter. Subscriptions to trade publications are often available at no charge, and one of the best resources we've found for them is TradePubs.com (*www.tradepubs.com*).

In addition to trade publications, you can learn a lot about your target audience by "lurking" on the e-mail lists they use. (For those unfamiliar with the term, an e-mail list or "listserv" is a subscriber-based forum where people can discuss a common interest by sending e-mail to a single address that, in turn, distributes the message to the entire subscriber base. "Lurking" means joining an e-mail list or other online forum and reading the communications without participating.) Once you've caught the rhythm and tone of the discussion and gotten a feel for the topic, you may decide to participate, making helpful (but non-promotional) posts as opportunities arise.

Many e-mail lists may be found at Topica (*www.topica.com*), but one of the best resources we've found—the topics cover almost anything you can imagine—is Yahoo! Groups (*groups.yahoo.com*). When you're there, simply enter the term you're looking for in the search box and select the lists your audience is most likely to be using. Some topics will be overly broad—we entered the search term *engineers,* for example, and received 5,303 returns—but you can narrow your search with more specific terms, such as *mechanical engineers,* which yielded only 328 returns.

Web-based message boards can also provide a useful "immersion environment." Unlike e-mail lists, however, where messages are sent to your e-mail in-box, message boards require that you log on and visit a given URL to make or review posts. One of their capabilities we like best is that you can easily track topics back over time to see how they evolved and what has been said on the subject since the beginning.

As with e-mail lists, there are many industry-specific message boards: a recent search on Google (*www.google.com*) using the term *"message board" engineers* yielded 341,000 returns. (Obviously, our search term again needs some refining!) Once you've located your message boards, we'd recommend the same approach you'd use with e-mail lists—lurk and learn for a while, then make useful, non-promotional posts. (We'll cover these in more detail in the next chapter.)

Industry-specific e-zines (magazines in electronic form) can also provide up-to-the-minute niche detail, because, as are their paper brethren, they're usually written for a target readership. Publishers distribute e-zines via e-mail or through designated Websites, and finding them is easy: Just use your favorite search engine. We entered the phrase *e-zine for engineers* (don't ask us why) in Google and discovered dozens of e-zines for all types of engineers.

The "immersion tools" we've mentioned here—trade publications, e-mail lists, message boards, e-zines—are not only great ways to get to know your target audience, but to market to them as well. In the next chapter, when we help you develop your Strategic Marketing Plan—your marketing road map to a successful client base—we'll show you how to use these same tools to deliver memorable and motivating messages to the best clients you can find.

CHAPTER 8

Let the Marketing Begin!

The leading cause of business failures among Virtual Assistants, by far, is ineffective marketing. Even a VA with the highest levels of skill and professionalism is destined to fail if no one knows she exists. That is why this chapter is the longest in the book. We wanted to give you as many useful tools and as much guidance as we could to help you succeed where too many, who really did not have to, fell short.

You've determined what services you'll be offering, how much you'll be charging, the niche(s) you'll target, and the profile of your ideal client. Now it's time to design and implement a focused, strategic marketing campaign to get the message to your prospects. It won't need to be complex or expensive, but it will require planning.

Before you begin to speak to your targets—by e-mail, phone, or mail, or face to face—you need a meaningful message and an image that reflects and reinforces it.

Defining "Brand You"

Solid VA-client partnerships—as are all good business relationships—are built on trust, and trust is based on performance. But it's unlikely you'll get the opportunity to perform at all if your image doesn't send the right message to your targets. Not to rub it in, but your mother was right: You really *do* only get one chance to make a good first impression.

As with other decisions in life, our senses play a central role in what we decide to buy. How an item feels, sounds, looks, or smells can have a tremendous impact on our purchasing behavior. And this makes selling intangibles such as services more challenging than selling shoes or tomatoes or leather coats. So how do VAs go about persuading people to buy the invisible? They start by projecting an image that creates an effective impression, an impression that invites (or, even better, compels) the prospect to take positive action.

Image Is Everything (Until You Have a Chance to Show Them the Rest)

You can tell prospects that you're "wonderful" and "highly effective" and that your work is the best thing north of the South Pole, but the bottom line is that you're asking a stranger to enter into a relationship with you based on appearances— image is all. But before you display this finished canvas of "You, VA," what will you paint on it? Which of your characteristics do you most want prospects to see? Honesty and professionalism? Efficiency and sophistication? Speed and cost-effectiveness? A professional palette has many colors. You'll need to choose the colors that suit you best, and combine them in the optimal manner on your "canvas" (your Website, stationery, brochures, business cards, and so forth).

And while we're on the subject of image, "borrowing" someone else's (unless you're in the forgery business) rarely works. The point is not only to land the client, but also to establish a long-term relationship with them, a relationship based on trust. Apart from the question of honesty and stress, sooner or later the image you've "borrowed" and the truth of who you are will collide, because you are unique. The moral? Choose an image that reflects the "unique you."

This image must also "capture and stimulate." Think for a moment about the products you see on the shelves of your local grocery store, the commercials on TV, billboards on highways, and ads you see in print. Each is designed to capture the attention of the target audience and stimulate a purchase. And again, there are many colors on the palette. For example, General Mills wanted its vitamin-packed Wheaties cereal to be as attractive to kids as it is to moms but understood that children find vitamins neither interesting nor desirable. So, in the mid-1930s General Mills began to put images of famous athletes and the slogan "The Breakfast of Champions" on the Wheaties boxes. Decades later the strategy is still working, so well in fact that it's not unusual to hear people say things such as, "Big game today...better eat your Wheaties!"

Though you won't actually be "sitting on a shelf" as grocery products do, you will be one VA among many, and it's important to stand out. To help loosen up the creative marketing muscles, we have students in our training sessions take part in the following "image visualization" and brainstorming exercise.

Imagine we've just handed you a large white "cereal box" and instructed you to create a VA package for you and your business. The design should project your image and hold a high level of appeal for your target audience.

✯ What do you envision on the front of the box, showcasing you to consumers as they walk down the aisle? (This is the composite that grabs the prospect's attention and makes him want to pick up the box and read the side panel.)

✯ Assuming you've succeeded in step one, what will he read among the "ingredients" on your side panel? For example: Ingredients: Effectiveness, Expertise, Competency, Proficiency, Commitment, Focus, Dependability, Value, Capability, Productivity, Trustworthiness, Reliability, Experience, Sense of Humor, Professionalism, Dedication.

✯ And let's not forget the back panel, often used to showcase special offers, or details about the "prize inside." What "little extras" do you have to offer your clients?

✦ First two hours free!

✦ Discounts offered for retainer clients!

✦ Canadian VA means your U.S. dollar goes farther!

✦ One hour free for every 15 hours paid!

✦ Secret decoder ring! (Kidding, but you get the point. Little extras can be "tie-breakers" when it comes down to you and the other VA finalists.)

Now you should have a better idea of the business image you'd like to project to your prospective clients, and maintain for them when they've signed up with you. Remember: At all points in the relationship, from first perception to goodbye, your performance should always be true to your image.

Talking About What You "Do"

The days of one-income families, sit-down dinners, country club weekends, and many more of what used to be dreams and hallmarks of leisured middle-class life have been steadily slipping away over the past few decades, unceremoniously replaced by escalating debt, work-obsessed weeks, and gnaw-ing doubts of upward mobility. And with the demise of gen-tler times, our social skills seem to have changed from respectful courtesy and circumlocution to cut-to-the-chase directness. (Imagine what our great-grandparents would have thought if they were milling about at a social gathering and a stranger approached them, thrust out her hand, and said, "Hi, I'm Mary Smith, consultant. What do you do?")

But take heart. As we're about to explore, although we may have lost some of our social graces, directness spells "mar-keting opportunity" for the confident Virtual Assistant—you—as long as you have a good answer to that vocational question you will surely hear. (Hint: "I am a Virtual Assis-tant," is a *not* a good answer.)

Writing Your "Elevator Speech"

What a high-speed world we now live in. The last ten sec-onds of the microwave's countdown take an eternity, traffic lights seem to stay red "forever," and we quickly grow irri-tated when the driver in front of us travels "only" at the posted speed limit. We're short on patience, time, and attention. The sound bite rules. And in the business arena, when you're trying to capture the attention of a prospective client, the "elevator speech" is your bite *du jour*.

The elevator speech (AKA "elevator pitch" or "martini monologue") is a brief distillation of a business or product, designed to compel the listener to ask for further information. The term derives from the hypothetical situation of a seller and potential buyer on an elevator together, with the seller having until the elevator reaches the buyer's floor—say, 60 seconds—to convince the buyer to consider doing business with her.

The elevator speech isn't a full-fledged sales pitch, but simply the "bait" on your marketing hook—for, as any fisherman will tell you, most fish will usually decide within seconds of the bait hitting the water whether they're going to nibble or flee. Consider the following conversations between Sandy VA (Virtual Assistant) and Mr. Bigshot (freelance writer and prospective client), and you'll see how one approach can lead to nibbles and another lead to, well, re-baiting the hook.

Scenario 1

Sandy VA:	"Hello, Mr. Bigshot. I've been hoping to speak with you about how I can help you."
Mr. Bigshot:	"Is that so? What is it you do?"
Sandy VA:	"I am a Virtual Assistant!"
Mr. Bigshot:	"I see. That's nice, but I don't think we need one of those."

(Uncomfortable silence. Elevator doors open. Sayonara, Mr. Bigshot.)

Scenario 2

Sandy VA:	"Hello, Mr. Bigshot. I've been hoping to speak with you about how I can help you."
Mr. Bigshot:	"Is that so? What is it you do?"
Sandy VA:	"I help busy freelance writers manage their non-core administrative tasks off-site, so they can focus on their writing, marketing, and other revenue-generating activities."
Mr. Bigshot:	"Hmm. I see. How do you do that?"
Sandy VA:	"Depending on their particular needs, I assist them with their research, scheduling interviews, editing and proofreading,

collections, accounts payable and, for those who have Websites, I even help them with site maintenance."

Mr. Bigshot: "Oh. I'd like to discuss this further. Do you have a business card so I can reach you?"

Sandy VA: "Of course, here you are. You'll find all of my contact information there and my Website address, too. In the meantime, may I send you an e-mail with an overview of my services, Mr. Bigshot?"

Mr. Bigshot: "Yes. I think that would be helpful. Thank you."

(Elevator doors open. Mr. Bigshot exits with Sandy's card in hand. Sandy, after the doors close, does the "happy dance" and hurries home to send that e-mail!)

In the first scenario, Sandy VA made a classic blunder by telling Mr. Bigshot what she "is" as opposed to what she "does." Her statement did nothing to spark his interest or stimulate further conversation. In a word, it was flat.

In the second context, Sandy had her hook properly baited. She immediately grabbed Mr. B's attention by telling him she specializes in working with his peers (and possibly his competitors) and that, with her assistance, they're improving their revenues and spending more time doing what they love (writing). Mr. Bigshot, too, probably wants to write more and do less non-writing business work, and he wouldn't be living up to his name (that is, his self-image) if he let Sandy's remarks pass without further investigation. ("If successful freelance writers have VAs, why don't *I* have one?") He then did exactly as Sandy had hoped—asking how she might help him— opening the door for the clinching points.

Based on the target markets you've selected, draft your own 60-second "elevator speech." Stay as close as you can to the "10-second lead-in, 50-second main theme" split we set up in Scenario 2. (Most busy people will pay attention for the first 10 seconds just to be polite. If you haven't given them a reason to keep listening by then, they probably won't.) As you draft your elevator speech, keep the following pointers in mind:

✯ Focus on what you do, not what you are.

✯ Concentrate on what matters to the prospect: their problems, pains, and predicaments, and how you can help.

✯ Let personal or professional strengths—your sense of humor, articulateness, special knowledge of the niche— shine through in your message. This can make the prospect want to connect with you on several levels.

✯ Create a list of benefits your clients will gain by working with you and include the most compelling of these in your speech.

✯ Keep your overall image in mind as you write your speech, and make sure it comes across.

✯ Consider possible resistance factors (lack of trust, no sense of need or urgency, money) and weave in language that will help avoid or neutralize them (for example, "I work with my clients to find solutions that will fit their individual budgets, whether they're booming or bootstrapping.").

✯ Practice, practice, practice. Make your speech to a tape recorder, your spouse, a mirror, your children—anyone who'll listen and give you their candid feedback. Relax. The pace should be natural and unrushed. Keep it spontaneous. If the speech sounds "canned," you'll lose your chance.

When you're ready, contrive to get yourself into as many "so, what do you do?" situations as you can. Let your words flow with energy and confidence! You have nothing to lose and everything to gain. Even if your prospect doesn't "bite," you'll have made a good impression on someone in your niche, and he or she may pass your name along to a colleague, media person, or other potential helper.

Marketing and E-Mail

Spam has become so bad these past few years that some people feel e-mail is no longer useful as a marketing tool. In our experience, this isn't yet true and, given the overall importance of e-mail to business generally, we really doubt that it will be. However, e-mail admittedly isn't as effective as it once was, which means you'll have to take even more care in handling yours to make sure you're getting your message across.

In its functions, e-mail remains the double-edged sword it always has been: a compelling, cost-effective, and informative platform for the good VA, and a booby trap waiting to explode for the careless. Nothing reveals us so quickly in the minds of most people as our language skills—"[S]peak that I may know thee," said the playwright, Ben Jonson—and apart from the occasional audio file or other attachment, e-mail is all language. Sloppy spelling and grammar, curt or imperial tones, and muddled thoughts won't leave the desired picture in our reader's mind's eye.

E-mail's enormous popularity among friends and family members can also lead to habits unsuitable to business correspondence. Slang, emoticons ("smiley faces" and so on), omitted apostrophes and hyphens, and "pajamas-and-bunny-slippers" phrasing can be fine for your brother or best friend, but they are clearly out of place with clients.

E-mail's lightning-quick turnaround is also a mixed blessing. (There's a reason that most fiction writers let their prose "cure" in a drawer or file before they send that final draft to the editor or agent.) The speed of exchange can almost approach the telephone's, yet the written word is a much different animal from speech. We perceive it differently, we absorb it differently, and it lasts forever.

2-Second Spotlight

E-Mail Etiquette Tips

Name:	Ann Marie Sabath
Business:	At Ease, Inc.
URL:	*www.ateaseinc.com*
Personal:	Ann Marie Sabath is the founder and president of At Ease, Inc., an 18-year-old firm specializing in domestic and international business etiquette programs. She is the author of *Business Etiquette: 101 Ways to Conduct Business With Charm & Savvy* and *Courting Business: 101 Ways for Accelerating Business Relationships* (both from Career Press).

Q: *What etiquette tips would you have for Virtual Assistants regarding e-mail with their prospects or clients?*

A: First of all, treat e-mail like phone calls: Answer promptly! When e-mailing prospective clients, use your message to develop permission-marketing techniques. Make your message "short and sweet," and include something that helps the reader see that you're more than just someone trying to make a sale. Your opening lines should include something that shrinks the distance and makes a connection with the reader, like a remark about the weather where he or she lives, or some local event or news item. • • • • •

Do's and Don'ts of Business E-Mail

✪ Reply promptly whenever possible (this projects an image of productivity and focus and shows the prospect that he or she is important to you).

✪ Keep your sentences short and to the point.

✪ Proofread carefully before clicking "send."

✪ Don't use HTML unless you know the recipient has compatible software. (Your background and special fonts may come up as gibberish on the other end.)

✪ Keep lines of text short. Scrolling from left to right to read a message is a nuisance. Sixty to 70 characters should be the maximum length of your lines.

Your Signature File: Your E-Business Card

E-mail "signature files" are a popular and reasonably effective passive marketing tool. A "sig file" is the online version of a business card, usually appearing at the bottom of an e-mail message, just after your "signed" name. On the following page are actual sig files used by practicing VAs.

Jen Rivet
Virtual Assisting Services
"Helping YOU Get On Course with YOUR Clients"
www.mymsva.com
E-mail: info@mymsva.com

• • • • •

Jana Young
Virtual Assistant/CEO Virtual Ease
(210) 522-9395 Phone/Fax
http://www.virtual-ease.net
"Virtually" behind you every step of the way!

• • • • •

Including your sig file at the bottom of every e-mail message and in your online posts leaves a lasting promotional and communications mark. Keep it short and informative. (Long sig files look vain or "salesy.") This is especially important if you post often to message boards, newsgroups and e-mail lists, because most groups have rules against blatant advertisements.

What Should a Signature File Include?

Include the basics—your name, business name, Website address, and, if you don't mind phone calls, telephone number. When communicating via e-mail, you can replace your e-mail address in your sig file with some other informative line, because the recipient will have your address in the "reply to" of the message. However, be sure to include it when posting to message boards and e-mail lists, as many of these won't provide readers with a way to respond to you "offlist." As for your physical address, you can usually omit it; people who receive a message online generally reply online as well.

Do you have a slogan or "tagline"—a one-line description of your services or solutions? If so, put it in your sig file as well. If you don't have a tagline, create one. It can be a powerful addition to your marketing arsenal, and you can use it in all your marketing materials. Just start with a list of "catch phrases" that you feel draw positive attention to what you do. Jot them down, even if they sound silly or hokey. It's amazing how often a concept can go from dull to brilliant—just mull it over and polish it a bit, and run it by a family member or friend.

Sandy Parks, owner of Jack Rabbit VA's, uses the tagline "Virtually the best staff you've never seen!" In addition to being a VA, Sandy is also a U.S. military spouse, making her one of a growing number of "MSVAs" (Military Spouse Virtual Assistants). You'll see in Sandy's sig file that she incorporates a simple graphic—an American flag created from normal keyboard characters—to show her pride in her MSVA status and let her prospects and clients know about it, too.

Sandy Parks
Jack Rabbit VA's
Virtually the best staff you've never seen!
http://www.jackrabbitsva.com
sandy@jackrabbitsva.com
```
* * * * * * = = = = = = = = = = = =
* * * * * * = = = = = = = = = = = =
* * * * * * = = = = = = = = = = = =
= = = = = = = = = = = = == = = = = =
= = = = = = = MSVA = == = = = = = =
= = = = = = = = = = = == = = = = = =
           • • • • •
```

Thankfully, the major e-mail applications (Microsoft Outlook, Netscape Messenger, Eudora, and so forth) let you create and store your sig file(s) once and add it automatically to the bottom of each outgoing message. You can use only one signature at a time, but you can create as many different sig files as you want and switch between them as your addressees change.

The process is simple. For example, in Outlook, you click on "tools" and, from the file menu, select "options" and click on the "signatures" tab. Then, in the "edit text" box, select "text" and enter the text for your signature. In Netscape, signatures are first created as "text only" or "text" files in a separate application. This can be done in the Notepad application (which saves as a .txt file automatically) or in Word (which saves as text only). Once you've created the signature, open Netscape and go to the "edit" menu, then select "mail & newsgroups account settings." Check the box next to the statement "attach this signature," then click on the "choose" button to browse your hard drive to select the file you created.

These are the basics of signature file creation but, by clicking on the "help" tab in your e-mail client, you will find full details for your specific program.

Your Website: A Global Billboard

Without a doubt, for most VAs the primary tool for reaching their target audience is the Website. The dry cleaners down the street may be able to get by without one but, for those in an industry where intangibles are sold at a distance, it's almost indispensable. (Granted, some VAs succeed without them, but we always suggest that they consider putting up at least a basic page or two, if only to have some place to send the media.)

The prospect of building a site can be daunting for those who've never done it, but it really isn't as hard as it seems. In fact, with a variety of WYSIWYG ("what you see is what you get") editors available, creating Web pages can be as simple as creating a document in your word processor. A detailed technical explanation of building a sophisticated site is outside the scope of this book—and in any case there's a wealth of expert guidance on the Internet itself and in bookstores and libraries—but we would like to share some basic information on Website construction and our thoughts on how to use your site optimally as a marketing tool.

Website Basics

First of all, make sure that everything you're thinking about putting into your Website will be consistent with your "offline" marketing materials. Colors, language, message, tone, approach—the "online you" and the "offline you" should be one and the same. (Remember that the key to good marketing is consistency.) Cross-promote, mentioning your hard-copy materials on your Website and vice versa. With good planning, your online and offline marketing materials will be seamless and will continually reinforce and support each other.

Now, to the geek stuff. In our training sessions, we've found that most new VAs are far less intimidated by Website construction once they get past the strangeness of the "geek speak" and discover definitions they can readily understand.

Here's a glossary of the common terms you may encounter as you go about building your site:

Domain Name: The unique name that identifies a Website. For example, Microsoft's domain name is "Microsoft.com"; ours is "Staffcentrix.com."

FTP: FTP, or File Transfer Protocol, is a standard means of sending files over the Internet. FTP programs (also known as FTP clients) are used to upload (send) the pages you create on your computer to the remote server where your site will be hosted. Using an FTP program is no more difficult than sending or receiving e-mail. It's simply a matter of knowing the address you are sending to and attaching the files you'd like to send. Two of the more popular FTP programs are Ipswitch WS_FTP (*www.ipswitch.com*) and GlobalSCAPE's Cute FTP (*www.globalscape.com*). Both offer a free evaluation and can be purchased for a reasonable price.

Hosting: Every Website is stored (hosted) on a server (a remote computer) that is connected to the Internet. These servers have the capacity, security, and software to store your Website pages and allow them to be viewed by the public when your domain name is typed into a browser. In short, the host houses your site, a service for which you will pay a small monthly or annual fee.

URL: The URL, or Uniform Resource Locator (commonly referred to as a "Website address"), is the unique address for any Web document.

WYSIWYG: As mentioned, WYSIWYG is an acronym for "what you see is what you get." These are the programs that have made Website construction accessible to everyone. (Before, site builders had to know how to write raw code, those odd-looking mixtures of commands, codes, and text.) Thanks to WYSIWYG programs, you can actually see what your final Web pages will look like as you create them. If you can use a word processor, you can create a Website using a WYSIWYG program. Microsoft FrontPage is one of the most popular, but you can also download Netscape's Composer (*www.netscape.com*) at no charge.

With these definitions in mind, and boiling it all down to its simplest terms, a VA brings her site to life on the Internet by:

1. Purchasing and registering her domain.

2. Selecting a host for her domain.

3. Creating her site using a WYSIWYG program.

4. Using the FTP program to "upload" her Web pages to the host server.

5. Giving her URL to everyone she meets!

Buying Your Domain

We recommend that every VA purchase his or her own domain as soon as possible, as it helps to establish your individual "brand." The cost of registering a domain varies greatly, with the more popular registration providers' fees ranging from $8.95 to $35. One of the registrars we've consistently heard good things about is GoDaddy.com (*www.GoDaddy.com*), where you can register your domain for less then $10 a year.

As an added benefit, GoDaddy offers reasonably priced hosting plans and tools for building your site. Other registrars we've heard good things about include Register.com (*www.register.com*), NameCheap (*www.namecheap.com*), and Dotster (*www.dotster.com*).

Once you've registered your domain, you'll need to find a host. (Remember that you'll be creating your site on your own computer, but, because the general population can't access your machine, you'll need to upload your pages to the host's server.) As with registrars, you'll find thousands of hosting options. If this is your first Website venture, we suggest that you host your site with the same company you used to register it. For example, providers including GoDaddy.com, Dotster, and Register.com offer hosting as well as registration services, which can simplify things greatly. If you're unsure which provider to use, consider asking your fellow VAs who they would recommend.

Using Free Sites While You Build Your Practice

For many VAs just starting out, buying a domain name and paying to have a site designed or hosted (or learning how to design and upload the site themselves) may have to be postponed until the practice is turning a profit. However, some sites will offer you a serviceable Web presence for free, and these are worth considering. For most, all you need do is register. The pages are generally easy to set up, and online support is usually offered, too. These sites provide a fixed amount of space, hosting, and a URL that you can refer clients to—the basics to get you launched.

One downside to the free hosting services is that your site may have to carry an advertisement (sometimes several) placed there by the host. Check out the hosts carefully to see which ones place the fewest ads or let you choose the ads that will appear on your site.

Among the better-known free site providers are Tripod (*www.tripod.lycos.com*), GeoCities (*geocities.yahoo.com*), and Zero Catch (*www.0catch.com*), but there are many others. For a comprehensive overview of free providers, check The FreeSite.com (*www.thefreesite.com/freewebpages.htm*). This site offers candid reviews of the various free hosting sites, and we've found that their assessments are usually quite accurate.

Site Content

Once the site set-up is taken care of, you can start to focus on content. (And again, don't forget that you'll be integrating your online and offline positioning.) To get the ideas flowing, spend some time browsing and researching other VAs' sites and make notes on what you like or dislike about them. Your "likes" list might include "fast-loading," "easy to navigate," "concise information," "friendly tone," and "welcoming colors." Your "dislikes" list might have "yellow text on a blue background," "slow-loading," "too much text on each page," and "no sense of the person behind the business."

As with all marketing initiatives, you should always keep your target audience in mind as you develop your content. Remember that your prospective clients are looking for a VA because they need help, and you should always assume they're in a hurry. Make sure your pages load quickly, your spelling and grammar are accurate, your information is fresh, and your message is meaningful. In short, leave your visitors feeling glad they stopped by to "see" you.

As with a paper-based marketing package, your Website should have multiple pages. We've all encountered sites made of one page that seems to scroll down endlessly. This layout makes it hard for visitors to grasp and assimilate your message and, if they're searching for something specific, it's not likely to leave them with warm and fuzzy feelings about your business.

We recommend that you start with your home page—no surprise—which functions as the site's foyer. It should be well organized and carry a warm tone, which will encourage visitors to explore other areas of your site. (This is the ideal place to create the image you envisioned for the front of your "cereal box" earlier in the chapter.)

Be sure your home page includes a site map or click-through index to the other pages (sub-pages) of the site. Following are some examples of sub-pages usually found on VA sites, followed by our comments:

✯ **"What Is a Virtual Assistant?"**
Use this page to define Virtual Assistance in a way that will be meaningful to your target reader.

✯ **"About Our Company"**
✦ Above all, "make it personal." The one thing that will distinguish your site from every other site is *you*. Put plenty of "you" (with a little polish, of course) onto this page!

✦ Include a photograph of yourself. (This is critical!) Potential clients will want to see who they're dealing with, and nothing personalizes a site the way a photo does.

✦ Keep in mind that this page functions as a resume, so treat it accordingly. Make sure the transitions are smooth and that the description of your company flows well. (As with any other content in your site, don't be shy in asking people whose judgment you trust to be your "beta testers" before you go live.)

✦ "Make the slope go *up!*" When you describe your company, accentuate your progress (whatever the details might be) as you sketch in the story. And be sure to end on a positive note!

✦ Let your enthusiasm come out with a confident, upbeat tone. This tells prospective clients that you bring energy and drive to your work. And as for confidence, everybody responds well to it.

✦ As with all content on the site, proofread, proofread, proofread. Make sure you've caught any typos, grammatical errors, or stylistic faux pas. (Again, it pays to have several people give your site a thorough vetting before you launch.)

✮ **"Benefits of Working With a VA"**
We explored these at length in Chapter 2. Review that information again as you draft your copy for this section of your site, but be sure to include industry-specific benefits that will speak directly to your target audience as well.

✮ **"What Our Clients Are Saying About Us"** (Testimonials)
Here you would include short, positive quotes from a few of your clients—with their permission, of course. (Don't despair if you're just starting out and don't have any testimonials yet and must omit this page; if you do your job well, they will come!) Also, when a client sends you an appreciative note or makes a glowing remark, consider putting it here. But again, don't forget to ask permission first!

(If you haven't landed your first client yet, you might also consider getting testimonials from former employers and changing the title of the page to something such as "Testimonials" or "What others are saying about us." Past employers can speak just as authoritatively as clients can to the issues of your performance and professionalism.)

☆ **"Our Promise to Our Clients"**

Use this section to tell your clients what they can expect from you and about your commitment to them. The "promise" page that Chris wrote for her Website back in 1999 read as follows:

In recognition of our professional obligation to our clients, we shall:

- Avoid conflicts of interest and insure that our client is aware of any potential conflicts.

- Present a fair, honest, and objective viewpoint.

- Protect the proper interests of our client at all times.

- Safeguard the privacy and confidentiality of all information entrusted to us.

- Refrain from using the resources of our clients for personal gain or for any other purpose.

- Accept full responsibility for work that we perform.

- Hold in the highest regard the authority entrusted to us.

- Represent truthfully information concerning the capabilities of our equipment, software or systems.

♦ Offer only those services that we perform well, and aid the client in finding assistance for the tasks that we are unable to perform.

★ **"Our Services and Fees"**

This is self-explanatory, though there's always been some debate as to whether VAs should post their fees to their Website. For our own part, we're the kind of shoppers who want to find prices on the things we're interested in. Co-author Chris says, "As a consumer, I'm far more likely to do business with someone who gives me all the basic information I need up front. Few things are more annoying than wandering around a car lot or store where there are no price tags on anything. The message in such places always seems to be that I don't have the good sense to make a buying decision without the guidance of someone on their sales team."

★ **"About Our Technology"**

Use this section to tell your prospective clients a bit about how your office is equipped. Include a list of hardware and software so they can determine whether your office and applications are compatible with their own and if you're equipped to handle their needs.

★ **"How to Contact Us"**

It may sound obvious, but don't forget to include your e-mail address here! (You may want to omit your mobile number, however, and save it for occasions when you can make the recipient feel "special" by scribbling it on your business card or including it selectively in your e-mails.)

And Update Regularly!

Periodic updates will keep your site fresh and interesting and will reassure prospective clients that there's a warm, alert "body" behind that Website.

But updates don't have to be complex or time-consuming; something as small as a niche-specific "tip of the week" can work fine. (If you do incorporate a "tip list," by the way, consider archiving the information on a separate page linked to your home page. It may not sound like much, but it lends depth to you and your site both and is one more useful thing to point to when you invite newsgroup or e-mail list readers to visit.)

Getting Noticed: Search Engines

The majority of your visitors are likely to find you through search engines and Web directories such as Google, AltaVista, Yahoo, and HotBot, so it's important to build your site in a way that helps their software find you. We won't get into the technical aspects of search engines, but let's review some basic steps you can take to improve site placement (positioning) in their results.

Keywords

Search engines scour the Net, looking for keywords within Websites that match the search terms a user has entered. Simply mentioning keywords somewhere in the text on your home page may occasionally suffice to catch their attention, but your chances will improve markedly if the keywords are actually written into your HTML (geek speak: HyperText Markup Language, the coded language used by Web designers to create Web pages). Again, this is not a complex process, and most WYSIWYG programs make it as simple as typing your keywords into the correct field.

Draft a list of the words or phrases your prospective clients are likely to use as search terms when they're looking for a VA. For most VAs, these would include *virtual, virtual assistant, assistant, virtual assistance, VA, virtual assist, virtual services, virtual staff, virtual support, online support, off site, office support, support services, administrative assistant, administrative, support staff, staff, executive assistant,* and *staffing solutions*.

You'll also want to include the more esoteric or specific keywords that apply to your specialty or niche. If you're targeting real estate professionals, for example, you'd include terms such as *real estate virtual assistant, real estate assistant, real estate forms, top producer, virtual tours, MLS, transaction management,* and so on.

As mentioned, search engines will also scan the text on your Website (in addition to the underlying HTML) and, if the search term appears frequently on any given page, many engines will rank that page higher in their returns. So in addition to listing your keywords in the appropriate place in your WYSIWYG program, you'll want to weave them into your site's content as well—but not to the extent that they sound ridiculous (I am a Virtual Assistant like no other Virtual Assistant so if you're looking for a Virtual Assistant I'm the Virtual Assistant you're looking for!). After all, search engine results are only as effective as the content they lead to.

Listing Your Site

Registering or "listing" with search engines can help make you visible quickly (though expect several weeks for your listing to take effect) and is one of the cheapest ways to increase traffic to your site. Registration basically involves going to the search engine's home page and looking for the text that says "Add URL" or "Add Your Site" (often found in the small print at the bottom of the page) and following the instructions. Be sure to submit the exact address of your site or profile page, preferably by going to the page you wish to register and copying the URL from the address field.

The process is simple but a bit tedious, so you'll probably want to start with just a few of the major engines and register with others as time permits. Some of the biggies are:

AltaVista	*www.altavista.com*
Excite	*www.excite.com*
Google	*www.google.com*
HotBot	*www.hotbot.com*
WebCrawler	*www.webcrawler.com*
Yahoo!	*www.yahoo.com*

Site Submission Services

If you'd rather leave the search engine registration process to someone else, there are many fee-based services that will help you, and we've listed some here. (We haven't tested or reviewed them, however, so we can't endorse or recommend any particular one.) Just key in your information once, and they'll register your URL with the search engines they feature.

Add Me	*www.addme.com/*
SiteMeter	*promo.sitemeter.com/*
Submit Express	*www.submitexpress.com/*
Submit It!	*www.submit-it.com/*
SubmitToday.com	*www.submittoday.com/*

Getting Noticed, Cont'd.: Posting to Newsgroups and E-Mail Lists

In an Internet-centric industry—and keeping the boot-strapping mantra in mind—it makes sense to use cost-effective Web options as often as you can to raise your site's visibility. Optimizing your site for search results and listing it with the engines is a start, but participating in newsgroups and e-mail lists can offer valuable results as well. (Web logs, AKA "blogs"—a personal or professional chronicle of events, more or less resembling a diary—have also become popular in recent years, but we have doubts as to how effective they are in recruiting VA clients. Most small-business people, in our experience, just don't have time to read them.)

Posting to Newsgroups

As we've mentioned, a newsgroup is an electronic bulletin board where people with shared interests can communicate. There are thousands of newsgroups on the Internet, with millions of daily participants. Done right and with care, posting to a newsgroup can generate sizeable—and almost instant—word of mouth.

If you opt to post to newsgroups, target only those that cover topics associated with your service. (Newsgroups for small businesses—the largest users of Virtual Assistants—are a great place to start.) But first, make sure the newsgroup accepts postings from newcomers. If it does, sit back and "lurk" for a day or two, to get a feel for the group's tone and unwritten rules. When you do post, don't advertise your service (a no-no), but offer advice or information in response to a query or an ongoing discussion.

Make your message specific and concise. Remember: You want to be helpful! Then you can close with a brief note that your site has useful information on the topic you're addressing or that you'd be happy to answer any further questions "offlist" (via separate e-mail).

Get your name out there and become a known participant by posting frequently with both advice and questions. (One of the basic tenets of newsgroups might be, "Give and Ye Shall Receive!") And don't forget to include your sig file at the bottom of your message.

Participating in E-Mail Lists

As we've said, an e-mail list is very similar to a newsgroup. The major difference is that messages go directly to a participant's e-mail box rather than to a central site or address. Our newsgroup suggestions apply to e-mail lists! And again, this is not an advertising platform—be cautious in your postings.

Launching With Fanfare: Press Releases

The actual launch of your VA practice—the day when you "go live"—is a PR opportunity that should not be missed. You'll want to get maximum impact from the "fresh news" that you and your company are now in the market. Major changes and upgrades to your practice may also present good opportunities for a press release.

A great deal has already been written on the creation and distribution of press releases, so we won't reinvent the wheel here. To learn all you need to know, simply go to your favorite search engine and enter "how to write a press release."

Better yet, enter "how to write a great press release." Adding "great" narrows the field considerably and will help you to help yours rise above the throng.

Harvesting the Local Business Crop

As you develop your practice, your client base may become national or international, and many of these clients you may never meet face to face. But just because you're virtual, don't forget the people down the street. VAs can often get off to a healthy start by marketing themselves to businesspeople they run into every week or every day or who do business just across town.

Prospecting locally can have many benefits. First, it lets people see who you are, which immediately removes the "trust" factor that virtual vendors must otherwise face. Second, you can often leverage an existing network—your local circle of family, friends, colleagues, and people you already do business with—rather than get bogged down establishing or expanding one online. Word of mouth can also work just as effectively, if not more so, in your local community.

There's a very good chance that many businesspeople in your community would benefit from your services if they knew you were offering them, so remember your elevator speech when neighbors, friends, or people you already do business with—dry cleaners, bankers, real estate agents—ask you what you do. Simply giving people the words to describe to others what you are doing can be an excellent way to get the word out and grow your business. Even if your listener can't use your services herself, there's a good chance she knows someone who can! (And be sure to carry plenty of business cards in your glove compartment, wallet, golf bag, diaper bag, picnic basket—you get the picture!)

Community Involvement: Building a Reputation in the "Right Places"

Getting involved in your community's civic or charitable activities can be a great way to build public relations and receive free publicity of the best kind. The old saying "you have to give to receive" holds just as true in business as elsewhere, so consider donating a bit of your time and talent where the community could benefit.

On the civic side, many smaller towns (in the United States), for example, depend on volunteers to help local government function. Often, the committees who deal with zoning, inland wetlands, recreation, and similar local issues need someone to take notes at meetings and return the minutes to the committee chair. Because these committees are usually made up of local business owners and other citizens who are well connected, this can be a great networking opportunity.

And while you're at it, why not kill two birds with one stone? Local papers usually want to report on the actions of town committees but often lack the manpower to cover every meeting. If you offer to contribute brief articles, you not only get your name in the paper, but may also receive a freelancer's fee.

On the charitable side, track the events in your area to see where your services might be of help and where exposure would benefit your practice. For example, if desktop publishing is your specialty, you might consider offering to lay out the programs for an upcoming play in the community theater.

Make sure that, in return for your hours of work, the organization would allow a credit line in the piece ("This program designed by..."), with your contact information. Similarly, when local business organizations sponsor events that feature a silent auction or service auction, consider donating a certificate that would entitle the winner to a given service (logo design, for example), or a few hours of your general administrative or other support at no charge.

Be creative! In your pre-VA days, you may have customarily overlooked many events in your community that may now offer the key to business development and earlier success!

An Idea From One of Our Favorite Local Marketing Stories

Several years ago we heard the story of a couple of active-duty U.S. military spouses who were helping each other get started in their VA practices and an interesting marketing idea they developed. We'll share it with you here so you can see how a little teamwork and imagination can lead to valuable results.

One VA specialized in database creation and maintenance, and the other had general administrative support skills. Together they decided to launch a "Messiest Office Contest," in which local businesspeople could submit a picture of their office and an essay on why their office was the messiest of all. The winner would receive an "office makeover" prize package.

The VAs wanted to make the prize package as attractive as possible, so in addition to their own services they lined up other donors with a promise of free PR. A local office supply store contributed a gift certificate, a local ergonomics expert donated a consultation, an office organization guru donated hands-on time, a rubbish removal company donated the use of a dumpster (for all the mess in the messiest office), and so on. In the end, it was a valuable array of services.

For the PR, the VAs approached a local radio station (most radio stations are open to offering prizes and contests on the air that relate to their market demographic), which liked the idea so much that they agreed to let their DJs act as the judges for the contest and offered to ask that essays and pictures be sent directly to the station for consideration. The DJs announced the contest regularly, including the names of the donors, components of the package, its value, and so forth.

The response was strong, and the radio station posted pictures of the messiest offices on its Website, so everyone got a good laugh. The contest had "staying power," too, as the station included "before and after" photos in the following weeks, after the winner received the donors' services.

The moral? Be creative! Opportunity often lies wherever you're willing to make it.

2-Second Spotlight

Free Publicity

Name:	Marcia Yudkin, Ph.D.
Business:	Creative Ways
URL:	*www.yudkin.com*
Personal:	Author of eleven books including *6 Steps to Free Publicity,* Marcia Yudkin is recognized as one of the world's top creative marketing experts. Her articles have appeared

in hundreds of magazines, including the *New York Times Magazine, TWA Ambassador, USAir Magazine,* and *Business 2.0,* and Marcia has been interviewed for and featured in a wide variety of business magazines.

Q: *What tips or advice for free publicity would you have for Virtual Assistants launching or already operating on a shoestring budget?*

A: Since the VA industry is still fairly novel, if you live in a small or medium-sized town you should be able to get some coverage by calling up a business reporter in the hometown paper and telling a bit about what you do.

You'll also want to think about your target industries—the industries you want to offer your services to—and the trade magazines for those industries. Write a simple, straightforward article on why the people or businesses in those industries might want to work with a VA. Assume that they don't know anything about Virtual Assistants; explain it in elementary terms. Then submit your article to the editors of those magazines.

● ● ● ● ●

Gaining Media Exposure to Build Your Practice

The media is a superb growth vehicle for VAs, but often it's overlooked because small-business people don't feel they merit coverage, or they think it's just too tough to get noticed.

True, getting media coverage isn't a "slam dunk," but it isn't as hard as it seems if you use creative and courteous techniques.

As you begin to weigh your own media options, here are some points to consider:

+ We have more media choices now than ever; it's a marketer's market. (This also means, of course, that those who are good at leveraging the media will have more opportunities to out-compete those who aren't.)

+ Media outlets today evolve and change more quickly than before, in part because of the Internet. Be sure to track your favorite media and keep up to date.

+ If you can name three media outlets that didn't exist 10 years ago, you know how rapidly the landscape can change. (Sample answer: Internet radio, satellite radio, Web-enabled cell phones.)

Now let's take a look at the "mediums that compose the media," and the pros and cons of each.

The Internet

As most people in the more "wired" nations know, the Internet, as a news distribution vehicle, is maturing. At first, the Web was a "content bonfire." Everything seemed to be considered newsworthy, and the pace of change was frantic. Now, the Net has generally become more selective (the bursting of the dotcom bubble accelerated this), and, apart from the larger news sites, content seems to stay longer on the page. On the variety side, many sites, again, have consolidated or gone out of business, and the remaining big-traffic news sites seem to parallel what happened earlier in regional radio and TV: They're all running the same "big story" items.

But that's the big picture. The fact remains that VAs can gain valuable exposure by contributing content—articles, opinions, columns, interviews—to selected Websites. The key word, of course, is "selected," because you'll want to be featured on sites that your niche audience not only frequents but respects and, even better, discusses!

And in the context of appropriate sites, we should also mention that many new VAs make the mistake of spending long hours writing content for sites, listservs, newsletters, and so on, that are targeted toward other VAs. Though it's important to network with your colleagues, and laudable to write things for the VA industry, are VAs your niche market? If not, your marketing efforts (particularly at the beginning of your practice) should probably be focused on reaching your prospective clients directly. Later, when you're in the black, you'll have time to write for other readers.

As you visit the sites devoted to your particular niche, and consider the form that your own contributions might take and how much time you'll devote to the Net as opposed to other media, you'll obviously have many variables to consider. For ready reference, we've summarized here some thought-starters and what we see as key aspects of writing for Websites and e-communications.

Pluses and Minuses of the Web as a Media-Marketing Vehicle

✦ The Web is still fragmented (a minus) but is consolidating around larger themes or subject areas (a plus; fewer sites means more exposure per item that you place or are mentioned in).

✦ The Web still lets you reach myriad markets or viewers globally with one item.

✦ Unlike magazines, Web-based content is still usually short-lived. This is bad (your item of today gone tomorrow) and good (your next item needed tomorrow!).

✦ "I'll be in the articles archives!" True, but will anybody go to the trouble of searching you out, or even know you're in there?

✦ Web-based-only publication carries more stature than a few years ago, but still not as much as an article or mention in a hard-copy publication.

Getting Featured on Portals: Is it Worthwhile?

✦ Some portals carry more weight than others.

✦ Is there high traffic, or low? Don't commit to large labor for small potatoes.

✦ Quality of traffic: Who will see you? Your target clients? Or miscellaneous surfers with no interest in your services?

✦ Monitor the portal for feedback on your item. Respond to negative comments (if any) constructively and calmly.

✦ When it's published on the site, double-check your item immediately for accuracy.

✦ Did the editor include your contact information?

Should I Write a Column for a Portal?

✦ What's the "bang for the buck"? Credibility? Exposure? Money?

✦ Beware of heavy time commitments. Good columns take work!

✦ "Re-purposing your property": Recycle your columns to other outlets or venues whenever permitted and appropriate.

◆ Include a good photo. "Always make it personal!"

You Are Where You Appear!

◆ Stay off sites that misposition you (the bad, the ugly, the irrelevant).

◆ Stay on "classy" sites!

Don't Forget Listservs and eNewsletters

◆ Many listservs carry news items.

◆ Several "small" listservs = many readers.

◆ eNewsletters always need news.

Don't Forget Regional Portals!

◆ Does your city or region have a portal that could feature you?

◆ Ideal for press releases.

As Always, Stay in Touch With Your Contacts!

◆ Keep your "media Rolodex" fresh.

◆ "May I keep you in the loop as things progress?" (This should be your standard close—with a "thank you"—to a written interview. No journalist ever wants to be "out of the loop.")

Keep a Record for Your Media Kit (the Collection of Key Information About You and Your Company That You Send to Writers, Editors, etc., to Persuade Them to Write About You)

◆ Print off the Web pages where you appear.

◆ Keep copies of articles you write.

◆ Build your media kit and keep it fresh.

Newspapers

Although we've since appeared in dozens of newspapers in the United States and around the world (*The Wall Street Journal, USA Today, The Christian Science Monitor, The Singapore Straits Times, The Australian, The London Times,* and so forth), we still remember vividly our first interview with a national (U.S.) newspaper. We were so excited, we couldn't sleep! We were too busy and impassioned by what we were doing to prepare, but when the big day came we answered all of the reporter's questions with lots of details and torrents of enthusiasm. The reporter was very sharp and took copious notes. However, when the article appeared a few days later, there were several major inaccuracies, and we couldn't understand how the points we had made could have been interpreted the way they were. In the end, we realized that the fault was ours. We had spoken far too rapidly, used obscure industry jargon, and given the reporter too much information rather than focusing clearly on the core themes of our story.

To help you weigh the pros and cons, here is an overview of newspapers as a media outlet.

Pluses and Minuses of Newspapers as a Media-Marketing Vehicle

✦ Short shelf life—here today, gone tomorrow.

✦ They confer credibility (with some exceptions, of course).

✦ They generally imply that "this topic is mainstream."

✦ In addition to other distribution channels, newspapers "lay around" and often pass through many hands (think Starbucks), increasing the odds that your story will be widely read.

As With Other Media, Research Your Publications: Their Content, Slant, and Readership

✦ Don't send an apple pie recipe to "Popcorn Eater's Daily."

✦ Don't talk about your love of cats to a dog editor.

✦ Don't try to sell meatloaf to vegetarian readers.

As With Other Media, Research Your Contact Person (Editor, Reporter) Before Writing

✦ What has he/she written before?

✦ Look out for quirks, passions, pet peeves.

✦ How does your "news" tie in with current and recent content?

Shoot for the Weekly Inserts (such as, "Smallville Business Supplement")

✦ Inserts and supplements are more targeted than the main paper.

✦ You'll get better "shelf life" and secondary distribution. Readers often keep inserts longer and pass them around, clip and send articles, and so forth.

✦ Inserts get singled out (whence their name).

✦ You'll get enhanced credibility through the "showcase" effect.

Letters to the Editor: Easy PR!

✦ Keep letters brief and succinct.

✦ Write with authority!

✦ Persevere!

Again, Think "Media Kit"!

✦ Keep copies of articles/items.

✦ Build your media kit strategically. (Don't submit material to newspapers or any other media haphazardly. Use published items and mentions as stepping-stones, going for ever-more-useful coverage.)

Monitor for Feedback on the Piece

✦ Watch out for negative feedback. Address it quickly, if you can.

✦ Feedback = response, and response = more exposure!

As Always, Keep in Touch With Your Contacts

✦ "May I keep you in the loop?"

✦ "Re our interview on home-based outsourcing last week, I thought you might be interested in this article about xyz from today's ZYX News."

Magazines

Magazines represent one of the optimal media outlets for VAs and other businesses: They generally offer high credibility, wide or targeted (niche) distribution, and a long shelf life. That said, they are also among the most difficult media to get into.

But there are different ways to thread the needle. As we mentioned earlier, trade publications can be a wonderful way in, because they bring your story directly to your target market, and they may be more receptive than mainstream publications to content shaped to your niche.

Whether you're authoring the article yourself or interviewing with a staff writer or freelancer, be sure to have a clear idea of what the readers want to read and what you want to cover, and stick to your topics or themes. Stay organized, be succinct, and nip tangents in the bud.

Following are some important considerations for VAs who would like to use magazines as a marketing tool.

Pluses and Minuses of the Medium

✦ Magazines offer far more positives than negatives. (Credibility and "persistent distribution" are invaluable.)

✦ Downside: Magazines often have long lead times before articles appear.

✦ You may find Iraq on the cover and yourself lost in a sidebar in the back. (It's harder to get significant placement in magazines.)

Except for the "Weekly Inserts," Our Bulleted Observations on Newspapers Apply!

✦ And as with newspapers, buy extra copies for promotional distribution.

Radio

Depending upon your niche, it can often be difficult to find radio programs and hosts that are right for you, and many VAs struggle with shyness, modesty, and other issues (though many of these can certainly be overcome) when they contemplate going on the air. However, some VAs have forged ahead to the mic and gained deserved exposure in their local markets, and we suspect that many more will follow as appearances become more prominent and as widely known hosts continue to discuss the industry (as Dr. Laura has done).

2-Second Spotlight

Tips for Getting on the Air

Name: Travis Dylan, Program Director

Business: LiteFM Norfolk, 92.1/107.7

URL: *www.litefmnorfolk.com*

Personal: Travis Dylan is the Program Director and afternoon drive Host at
Norfolk's LiteFM radio. A Navy
veteran from a distinctively military
family, Travis has led a number of
initiatives in support of military
families generally in the Hampton
Roads area. He lives in Virginia
Beach with his wife, Kristen, their
dog, Buzz, and Buzz's two sidekick
cats.

Q: *How would you suggest that VAs approach their
local radio station to land an interview?*

A: The first step is to match the topic or product with
the correct format, which is the music or other
programming the station carries. Think about the
typical listener of the stations in your market and
ask yourself, "Does my service or topic target that
person?" Once you've zeroed in on the right format,
take the time to ensure whatever it is you're pitching
is (1) compelling and (2) entertaining. Radio hosts
and producers strive for a seamless blend of
information and entertainment, so be prepared to
"make the phones light up"!

One of the most challenging tasks is to find the
decision maker, who is usually the program director,
show producer, or in some cases the host. Once you've
got that information, be tenacious. Don't be disappointed

if your calls aren't returned; keep trying. At the very least, try to develop some sort of dialogue so you can follow up and eventually get on the air.

Once you've been granted the interview/air time, *always ask for an aircheck* (a recorded segment of your appearance). This is vital, as you'll use it to build your resume so that other prospective stations have an idea of just how compelling and entertaining you are.

To get started, you can usually find a listing of your local radio stations in the yellow pages. (Online you can use a search engine, but for access to a national directory of stations you may have to pay a subscriber fee, and the directory may or may not be up to date, so beware.) Get the call letters and find the front desk number (avoid the request line). In most cases the front desk operator knows more than anybody else in the building!

Helpful Hint: Radio is required by law to serve the community. Most stations do this by featuring a Public Affairs show in one form or another, and they tend to be the hungriest for good local guests.

• • • • •

For VAs contemplating radio, we'll include here a few more key points to consider.

Pluses and Minuses of the Medium

✦ Radio has little "persistence" compared to most print media.

✦ Radio is a high "content burner"—many stations, many hours of airtime to fill every day, without fail. You and your story are content.

✦ Radio is a more "glamorous" medium than print, hence competition for exposure on all but the smallest shows may be ferocious.

✦ You can reach a large audience with relatively modest effort.

✦ Radio usually confers less credibility than print media.

✦ You can polish a print piece to perfection but, once you're at the mic, you're "on." And if you're live (which is often the case), a blunder can't be recovered: You can't unring a bell.

Be Careful: Voice Is a Wild Card

✦ If you sound like SpongeBob, you'll "look" like him, too (in the listener's imagination).

✦ Tape yourself and get objective feedback before you commit yourself to a radio initiative.

Call-In Shows Often Work Best

✦ Demonstrate your expertise.

✦ Prospective clients will call.

Again, Except for the "Weekly Inserts," Our Bulleted Observations on Newspapers Apply!

✦ But in place of promotional copies, don't forget your aircheck!

Tips for Working With the Media

Regardless of which media outlets you choose to pursue, there are certain steps you can take to help ensure your success.

General Do's and Don'ts

✯ Know your addressee or telephone target thoroughly before you initiate contact.

✯ Don't waste your target's time. Be brief and clear (think sound bites) and always honor deadlines.

✯ Personalize your communications.

✯ Respect "no" and be prepared for it. Turn it into a positive: What was it about the story or pitch that doesn't fit? Is there someone else they can suggest for whom the topic might work better?

✯ Be persistent, don't badger, and don't be offended by "no." You yourself didn't get the thumbs-down, your pitch or story did.

✯ Be likeable. (*Was* it you who got the thumbs-down?)

✯ Regard your contacts as a resource and investment for the long haul, not the quick fix.

Interview Preparation Checklist

✯ Gather information about the publication or program.

✯ Learn all you can about the reporter or host.

✯ Set communications objective(s) for the interview.

✯ Make a list of ideas that could lead to good dialogue.

✯ Create a list of questions you do and *do not* want to answer, and develop short answers to each (not to serve as a locked-in script, but as a thought-tickler).

How to Give "Good Answers"

The purpose of a media interview is to achieve your communication objective(s) by getting your message through the reporter to the audience. It always pays to construct good answers—the message you want to send—before you sit down to an interview.

You are more likely to be quoted accurately and positively if your answers:

✦ Reflect your communications objective.

✦ Follow a pyramid-like structure (objective first, then supporting information) or a story-like construction (a beginning, middle, end, punch line, moral, and so forth).

✦ Emphasize benefits rather than features.

✦ Avoid jargon.

Your Post-Interview Review

After every interview, take a few minutes to analyze the dialogue, while everything is still fresh. Ask yourself:

✦ Did I accomplish my objective?

✦ What else did I accomplish?

✦ What follow-up is needed and when?

✦ What questions were asked that I didn't expect? How did I answer them?

✦ How could my answers have been more effective?

A Little Excitement Goes a Long Way!

Being a successful VA is hard work, and the early stages of your practice will be the most stressful time of all. If you land some media exposure—and there's no reason whatsoever that you can't—let it be the reward it ought to be. It's exciting to see your name in print, or hear it on the air. Let yourself go and enjoy it. Share it with family and friends, and drink your champagne with a smile.

We should never let ourselves become so tired or jaded that we can't enjoy the triumphs we've earned. Work hard, share joys, and be good to yourself!

Writing Testimonials for Free Exposure

When you're looking for ways to build traffic to your Website, or you're searching for additional hard-copy exposure, a well-placed testimonial can often do the trick, and earn you a useful "chit" as well.

On the Web: "Job Well Done" = Links Well Done

Everyone with a Website knows the importance of ranking high in the search engines. Among other criteria, the engines tally the number of links leading back to your site. "Reciprocal links"—I link to you, you link to me—are the usual solution, but they can create a distracting and unfocused Website. A better way is through testimonials.

Next time you're using the Web and find a site you like, check to see if it has a testimonial page. If so, take the testimonial template we're about to help you write, tweak it for the site in question, and e-mail. Like you, most business owners love to post testimonial letters, and if you're lucky you'll get a link back to your site.

For your testimonial:

✦ Be concise but creative. You want your note to stand out.

✦ Tactfully word your letter in a way that will motivate readers to visit your site.

✦ Don't say anything you don't believe. Your credibility is far more important than a mere link from a site.

Sample Letter

The following might be sent to a site for a graphic design service:

> I'm the CEO of XYZ Virtual Marketing Associates, Inc., and understand the challenges that Internet-based businesses can sometimes face even now when asking customers or clients to purchase services. "Will the service turn out to be what I hoped and trusted it would be?"
>
> Whether we're purchasing graphic design for ourselves or on behalf of a client, we know that PQZ Graphics can produce just what we had in mind, and get it there on time. Your professionalism and dedication to cost-effective service mirrors and supports our own, and consistently delights our clients.
>
> Thank you for your excellent service. You've given our busy office one less thing to worry about.

• • • • •

(Be sure to include your name, practice name, URL, and contact information.)

It takes only a few minutes to send a testimonial, and the cumulative results can be well worth the time.

On Paper

Ever walk into a car dealership and read the testimonials on the bulletin board as you're waiting for your car to be fixed? Or do the same thing at a florist, or dry cleaners, or car wash?

Keep your eyes open for places where your own letterhead might fit. Depending on your practice area, you may well find a location where you'd like to get some free exposure, and many small businesses see much more traffic than you might guess.

Marketing Through Guest Lecturing

Appearing as an expert in some aspect of virtual services— be it in your specialty, or in "home shoring" or outsourcing generally—can be an excellent way to showcase your practice, meet potential clients, and generate positive word of mouth. The phenomena of Internet-enabled, home-based careers and virtual business support are still quite young, and many organizations would welcome the chance to enlighten their members or "constituencies" on what these trends might mean for their businesses, careers, or family lives.

Colleges, Universities, and Business School Opportunities

One way to get free exposure is through an appearance as a guest lecturer at your local community college, business school, or "adult ed" organization. Many institutions publish their catalogs online, and a little research will tell you the titles and instructors of courses that you might contribute to. Teachers are always looking for good material and guests to supplement their curriculum, so a friendly e-mail to the instructor with an offer to come in and say a few words (or appear in an online forum) is likely to get a positive response.

Business and Professional Organizations

And as with other aspects of client development, don't forget the conventional opportunities down the street. Rotary clubs, chambers of commerce, Toastmasters, and even economic development get-togethers at the local library can offer you valuable opportunities to strut your stuff and share some of your latest-word expertise. (Don't forget, of course, that some groups won't spend nearly as much time on the Internet as you yourself might, so avoid trying to dazzle these audiences with your command of the latest e-tools and the e-future. You want to educate, assure, and win hearts and minds, not raise the specter of overwhelming change.)

2-Second Spotlight

Speaking Engagement Etiquette Tips

Name: Ann Marie Sabath

Business: At Ease, Inc.

URL: *www.ateaseinc.com*

Personal: Ann Marie Sabath is the founder and president of At Ease Inc., an 18-year-old firm specializing in domestic and international business etiquette programs. She is the author of *Business Etiquette: 101 Ways to Conduct Business With Charm & Savvy* and *Courting Business: 101 Ways for Accelerating Business Relationships* (both from Career Press).

Q: *What etiquette advice would you have for VAs giving presentations and attending business mixers at their chamber of commerce, Rotary, and similar business organizations?*

A: When attending any networking function, recognize that you are in effect a "walking billboard," a walking advertisement for your business. You should also dress one notch above the client you're trying to attract. In other words, if your target client is going to dress business casual, you should be wearing a black tailored suit, or a jacket and tie. Also keep in mind that the bona fide decision-makers are going to be dressing *up* a notch or two above the "average Joe."

• • • • •

"Upselling" Existing Clients

Although many VAs, as do most businesspeople, will want to continue to expand their client base, there's a lot to be said for marketing (gently) to existing clients. Not only is it far cheaper than landing new clients, but it takes much less effort: Existing clients trust and rely upon you and are usually loath to change.

To get started, take a look at your client list:

✦ How many clients are still using you only for the services they first hired you for?

✦ Are they knowledgeable about the other services you offer? (Don't assume they are, and don't assume they don't need them!)

Obviously, you'll want to avoid aggressive marketing tactics, but there are softer approaches that should be acceptable.

One possibility might be a brief e-mail to poll clients on the services they need most. Here's a sample query:

> In our continuing effort to provide the best service we possibly can, we know that the most important information comes from you—our clients.
>
> To that end, we'd like to ask if you would take a moment to review the list of services we offer and indicate the ones you feel might be of value to you now or in the near future. Also, please let us know what services we might add to meet your needs more effectively.
>
> We know the value of your time, and in exchange for your completed reply we will be pleased to credit one-half hour of our customary service to you on your next statement from XYZ Virtual Consultants.

● ● ● ● ●

An unobtrusive e-mail or note not only reminds your clients of the full range of services you offer, but it shows them you care about their opinion and their time and about their relationship with you.

Our 5 Favorite Marketing Tips

Over the years, working with thousands of VAs worldwide, we've explored and exchanged countless marketing ideas, because *landing the business* is so important to a VA's survival and success. What works? What doesn't? Here are five of our favorite approaches.

1. The "weenie on a toothpick."

2. Marketing to downsizing companies.

3. Replying to classified ads for "employees."

4. Marketing to expanding startups.

5. Marketing to regional hotels.

1. The "Weenie on a Toothpick"

If you've ever shopped at one of those big warehouse stores where the shopping carts are as big as Volkswagens and everything is sold in industrial-sized containers, you've probably seen white-frocked salespeople stationed at the end of the frozen food aisles offering customers food on toothpicks.

The shoppers sniff, examine, and nibble, and, if they like what they taste, they make their way to the freezer and load several boxes into their cart.

Free samples are an old favorite of smart marketers. If your sales are flat or you want to jump-start your marketing, we suggest giving promising prospects the first two hours of your service for free. Do a fantastic job for them, and they'll want to "fill their cart" with you.

2. Marketing to Downsizing Companies

Nobody likes to hear news of layoffs. One can't help but sympathize with the many families and individuals who are affected and the company's misfortune. But as in nature, every business sector has its cycles, and opportunities arise in the process.

Downsizing companies often find themselves short-handed and turn to outsourcing to help them through the transitions. Monitor the media for announcements of corporate contractions and staffing changes, and send your marketing kit to the hiring party. (Keep in mind that companies in quick-shrink mode are likely to be stressful and distracting environments, so keep your information short, sympathetic, and clear, and be prepared to be persistent.)

What do you say in your letter? Depending upon your practice, you might send something along these lines:

> At AZB Virtual Assistance, we know that rapid changes in personnel and operations can wreak havoc with workflow and productivity, and it's often hard to gauge exactly how much administrative support will be needed once the new configuration is in place. Unfortunately, this can mean that your administrative staff is running flat out (or struggling with low morale) as it tries to keep pace with fluctuating needs. Operations can stumble, revenues decline, and the entire mission can be put in jeopardy.
>
> Our "instant-on" administrative support services may well hold the solution you need, when you need it. When administrative demands outpace your team, or new circumstances threaten to undermine your executives' performance, we're available to power you forward, for the long haul or the sprint—without termination headaches, employee downtime, or unemployment issues. And when you need us again, we're ready to hit the ground running—just an e-mail away—having already learned, in the trenches with you, your company's needs, goals, and unique culture.

• • • • •

Close warmly and include an "action" note (such as "I'll contact you...") and a brochure, and you're good to go.

3. Replying to Classified Ads for "Employees"

When prospecting for clients, read the classifieds. It may sound odd, as you're not seeking "employment," but companies who are looking for an employee can sometimes be sold on an outsourcing solution, particularly when you can explain the many savings the offsite alternative can bring.

Instead of sending a resume, send a letter, telling the company how you can handle the advertised responsibilities and other tasks. Be sure to include your customary compelling prose on the benefits of working with an offsite expert, and, if the company is within face-to-face distance, say you'll be calling shortly to discuss the opportunity and your indispensable solution in more detail and that you look forward to meeting them.

4. Marketing to Expanding Startups

Startups—when they've been operating for a bit and are hitting their growth marks—can throw off sizeable streams of work, far more than any single VA could handle. Better still, these "newborns" or toddlers are often suffused with innovative thinking and bold personalities, and a proposal that might strike the manager of a stodgy old "blue chip" as patently unworkable may well set the startup's CEO or VP afire.

News of expanding startups can be found in many outlets. Among the magazines, *Business 2.0, Inc., Fast Company, Fortune Small Business,* and others carry news in hard copy or on their Websites about growing young companies, often including profiles of key executives.

Similarly, the business sections and weekly inserts in larger newspapers will often cover the area's growing young companies, and with a Google search or two you can find additional interviews with founders or investors who can give you valuable insights into how the company functions and where they want to go.

And there'll be other signs of growth or opportunity. For example, check your local or regional newspaper for news of appointments to boards of directors, hiring news ("Clark Kent Named Widget's VP of Sales"), funding announcements ("Widget Secures $2M in Second Round of Financing"), and news of new offices ("Anaconda Technologies Opens New Office in Duckburg").

Online, you can find reams of breaking news about defense and other federal and state contracts being awarded to smaller companies, each item a growth sign and potential opportunity for the committed and enterprising VA: you!

5. Marketing to Regional Hotels

Hotels around the world host or lodge untold thousands of harried businesspeople every week. Often, these beleaguered guests and visitors find that they need a critical letter, memo, or report—or some other life-threatening task—done "by tomorrow morning." Because few of these folks have ready access to administrative or related support, they often end up burning the midnight oil and otherwise assaulting their jet-lagged minds in an effort to pull the project together themselves. What happens the next day? What should have been a sharp and effective sales call or appearance on an industry panel becomes a forgettable or even damaging flop.

Contact the managers of the hotels in your area and go in and tell them about your services. Let them know you're readily available to assist harried businesspeople reliably and professionally on an as-needed basis, and ask them to add you to their "menu" of business services. (And if you can work on-site from time to time, tell the managers of the larger hotels that you're available to assist conference groups who may need to have notes or tapes transcribed for distribution by the end of their event.)

Your "Strategic Marketing Plan"

Now it's time to bring your marketing thoughts, insights, and projections under one handy umbrella: your Strategic Marketing Plan (SMP). The SMP helps you establish and co-ordinate your marketing efforts, energy, and funds. The process of writing your SMP will force you to assess your marketplace comprehensively and determine the steps you must take to bring clients to your table. The SMP will also serve as an assembly point for much of the information you have developed so far.

To put the SMP in context, in our heretical opinion the SMP is often more valuable to the new VA than a conventional business plan, those elaborate road maps that so many advisors, agencies and other authorities recommend. Why? Three reasons:

1. Most VAs who fail, as we've said, do so from weaknesses in marketing.

2. VA businesses are typically one-person microenterprises, most often intended to generate supplemental, not principal, income, without recourse to third-party funding (where a business plan would be required).

3. VAs who land clients early tend to succeed, and the longer a VA struggles to sign that first client, the more likely she is to go under.

New entrepreneurs often get bogged down and lose precious momentum and passion in the minutiae of business plans. We say it's often better to hit the ground running with an SMP and grab that first client as soon as possible. Our mantra is *Get Black Ink, Get Black Ink, Get Black Ink!*

Structure and Content of the SMP

The SMP is made up of several sections, which we'll introduce and summarize here before exploring them in more detail, when we turn to the outline of a sample SMP. Refer back to these introductory notes as needed when you review the outlined sample and begin to put together your own SMP.

The "Core Marketing Message"

At the heart of effective marketing is a message that addresses the needs of your prospective clients. This will be the copy that you include in your written marketing materials, as opposed to what you would say when speaking to prospects in person. Answering the questions you'll find in this section will aid you in the development of a powerful marketing plan.

Verbalization of the "Core Marketing Message"

You should answer the questions you'll find in this section in "sound bites," to get comfortable in using them as responses in face-to-face dialogues with prospects. If you've written your elevator speech, you may find that you've already done most of the legwork for this section.

Client "Benefit Statements"

It's critical to establish an intimate understanding of the needs of your clients. How will your customer profit or otherwise gain from using your services? Benefit statements will often point out what the client will *save* (money, time), *increase* (income), *improve* (productivity), or *reduce* (expenses) as a result of your services.

Market Analysis

As we've emphasized, your marketing efforts will be most effective when you gear them toward *specific target markets*. The more you know about your prospective clients, the better you can connect with them. Who will benefit the most from your knowledge and services? In this section you'll list those "niche" markets you identified earlier, the markets you're most qualified—and want—to help.

Selection of Key Marketing Vehicles Based on Your Target Market(s)

Looking at your target markets, list the marketing vehicles that you've determined will be most effective in reaching each. Before adding any marketing vehicle to your list, however, be sure you've answered these questions:

✦ Will this vehicle reach enough of my prospects to justify the effort in using it?

✦ Will it reach prospects when they'll be most receptive to my message?

✦ Will this marketing vehicle enhance my message?

Assess each of your target markets individually and list the specific outlets you'll be using to reach them. Which newspapers, magazines, trade publications, radio programs, Websites, or events do you intend to pursue?

Marketing Promotional Strategies

This section includes a series of questions about steps you'll take to network, encourage referrals, and gain credibility.

Exposure Through Speaking and Writing

Here you'll expand on written and oral venues and material you plan to use to reach your target audience(s).

The Million-Dollar Question

You'll wrap up your SMP with your answer to one of the most important questions an aspiring Virtual Assistant can ask.

Following is the outline of a comprehensive SMP. Where appropriate, we've included sample text and tips (in italics) to help spark your creativity and kindle the writing process.

Strategic Marketing Plan Outline

Core Marketing Message

1. Who are you?

   XYZ Virtual Assistance is a full-service Virtual Assisting practice, founded on the knowledge that small businesses can grow faster and more intelligently with professional support. Smart businesspeople use quality providers of administrative support services as trusted allies and growth partners.

   XYZ is such a vendor. We serve our clients as a trusted ally, providing them with the loyalty of a business partner and the cost-benefits of an outside vendor.

2. What solutions do you provide?

   We work with businesses to determine first which non-core administrative tasks they are spending time on—tasks that don't contribute directly to the growth of the concern. We then manage these non-core tasks off-site, so clients can focus on the areas of their businesses that stimulate revenues, profits, and growth.

3. What kinds of people and businesses do you work with?

   Our clients are solo entrepreneurs and small businesses who wish to increase productivity without increasing staff.

4. What are your clients' relevant needs (their problems, pains, or predicaments)?

   Our target clients are successful businesspeople who have reached a point where administrative burdens are hampering their growth. They are looking for a qualified professional to handle this workflow, so they can regain time for business development, marketing, and other rewarding activities that induced them to go into business in the first place.

5. What sets you apart from your competitors?

   We have built an excellent reputation for quality work both for individuals and small businesses. We continually strive to provide services that our clients value and need, and that meet or exceed their expectations—in every detail. Our commitment to client satisfaction is second to none.

6. What are the primary benefits a client receives through your services?

   We save our clients time, money, and anxiety by "partnering" with them to act as an extension of their own business, and we provide customized solutions for their administrative support needs. Clients receive critical professional services on an "as-needed" basis, with none of the costs or obligations associated with on-site staff.

Verbalization of Your Core Marketing Message

When someone asks what you do, how do you respond? Try to break your response into four parts:

1. Who is your target market? Tell the listener how your service is for them!

   "I work with entrepreneurs and small businesses..."

2. Touch the problem, pain, or predicament your target market is experiencing.

   "...who have reached a point where too much of their time is consumed with routine administrative tasks that get in the way of business growth."

   Wait for a response or question.

3. Tell the listener about the solution you offer to the problem you just cited.

   "I manage their non-core administrative tasks off-site, so clients can focus on the areas of their businesses that stimulate revenues, profits, and growth."

4. Then tell him/her what makes you different from your competitors.

   "I've built an excellent reputation for quality work both with individuals and small businesses."

Client Benefit Statements

In this section, list the top three unique benefits your services will bring to your clients, and draft a statement that conveys these advantages to your audience. *Remember to focus on what your client will save (money, time), increase (income), improve (productivity) or reduce (expenses) as a result of using your services.*

Benefit #1:   *Time savings*

Communication:

Business should not be an inherently do-it-yourself proposition; however, many small-business owners find themselves juggling administrative chores to the detriment of growth. Our as-needed professional support services will relieve you of all your administrative tasks and free you to spend time on profit-generating work, the things that attracted you to your business in the first place.

Benefit #2:

Communication:

Benefit #3:

Communication:

Market Analysis

My primary target markets are:

1. *Real estate agents*

2. *Tax lawyers*

3. *Movie stars*

4. *Successful motivational speakers*

5.

Selection of Key Marketing Vehicles

To reach target market 1, I will use the following vehicles:

Newspapers:

Anytown Tribune (Sunday Real Estate section)

Trade Publications:

Connecticut Real Estate Journal, The Real Estate Weekly, Realty Times

Radio Programs:

Jim Smith's Real Estate Hour

Magazines:

Real Estate Professional Magazine

Web Portals:

Homes.com, National Association of Hispanic Real Estate Professionals

Events:

National Association of Realtors Conference, Anycounty Real Estate Conference

Follow this process for all of the target markets you have identified.

Marketing Promotional Strategies

Referral Strategy

1. How can I leverage my good reputation and existing network of colleagues, friends, and satisfied clients for references that will help build my practice?

2. How and when will I ask for referrals and testimonials so my clients will be willing to provide them?

3. How can I best acknowledge and reward referrals?

Networking Strategy

1. How can I leverage networking activities to attract new clients?

2. What groups will I join to gain visibility and credibility?

Exposure Through Speaking and Writing

1. How can I gain exposure and credibility through public speaking and writing?

2. What are some key topics that are likely to be of interest to my target audience?

The Million-Dollar Question

What will I do to build the kind of loyalty in my clients that cannot be eroded by distance or competition?

I will under-promise and over-deliver at every opportunity, always meeting or surpassing my clients' expectations. Customer satisfaction will be a top priority for me. I will act to identify and anticipate the needs of my clients and will make sure they feel uniquely important and appreciated.

• • • • •

Marketing Wrap-Up

You should always consider your SMP a "work in progress." Don't let its written form fool you: It's a living extension of your practice, to be revised or "pruned" regularly to reflect changes in your niche, expertise, competition, media path, and so on.

Even more importantly, remember that writing and tending to your SMP is only half the equation: Your Plan is only as effective as your efforts. Stay focused on the steps you've outlined, and take them in increments that feel right for you. Keep track of the people you contact, the actions you take and their results, commitments that have been made to you or that you've made to others, and deadlines you've set for achieving each of your marketing goals. Step into the marketing arena with the boldness and determination to achieve your dreams, the good sense to know that some will be harder to realize than others, and the flexibility to adapt when the situation warrants.

CHAPTER 9

Pulling It All Together and Keeping It There

In this chapter, we'll focus on the final, pivotal challenge in all "virtual" relationships—collapsing the distance between the parties—before concluding with some parting tips and thoughts on making your practice a success.

Making "Virtual" Disappear: Creating a Sense of Shared Space

As a Virtual Assistant, you'll often find yourself extolling the virtues of remote partnering: explaining to prospects that a relationship with you can be as seamless, effective, and smooth as an on-site arrangement. Once you've sold the "sizzle," however, you'll have to bring the steak, making good on these promises when the client says yes. You are the "virtual professional" in the partnership, and in most cases your clients will be looking to you for guidance when it comes to effective offsite collaboration.

Because most brand-new VAs have never experienced a fully virtual working relationship, it's natural for them to have some concerns about their new role of "virtual collaboration expert." Thankfully, however, collaboration tools have become readily accessible and easy to use, so, even if you're feeling a bit apprehensive, you can become adept at using a variety of tools in a very short time.

Instant Messaging

Most Internet users have used some type of instant messenger (IM) to communicate with friends and family. Similar to e-mail, instant messaging involves sending text messages over the Internet. However, unlike e-mail (which is sent quickly, but often sits in the recipient's inbox for a bit before being read), instant messaging permits "real-time collaboration" (RTC), allowing for the rapid exchange of spontaneous thoughts and dialogue as fast as the participants can type (or, in the case of speech recognition software, speak).

There are many IM utilities (most of them free), and most have capabilities that reach beyond instant text messaging, including file exchange, conferencing, speaking over the Internet, and Web cam connections. To find the one that suits you best, field-test the likeliest candidates with a friend—rather than on that first client!

Instant Messaging Utilities

AIM (AOL)	*www.aim.com*
ICQ (I seek you)	*www.icq.com*
MSN Messenger	*messenger.msn.com*
X-IM (encrypted)	*www.x-im.net*
Yahoo! Messenger	*messenger.yahoo.com*

A word of caution: Train your clients from the outset to use the IM only for matters requiring your immediate attention.

Otherwise, because many of your clients may also be solo professionals, as you are, yearning for a bit of human interaction, you may soon find yourself interrupted with such attention-grabbers as, "Boy, I sure could go for a burger!" and "Have you heard this one?? A duck walks into a bar..." (and even the duck joke will be non-*bill*able). Most IM programs also have an option that allows you to show yourself as "online, but busy," so when your client-obedience training weakens, you'll still have a courteous shield.

Finally, remember that most IMs aren't secure. If yours doesn't have an encryption feature, be sure to avoid sending sensitive or confidential information.

Faxing

Faxing may not be as hip as it once was, but most VAs will still want to be able to receive faxes, for that occasional piece of paper that can't be sent to them any other way. If you don't have a fax machine now, however, and you don't expect to be sending many hard-copy faxes short-term, you can keep your initial costs down by using Internet-based fax services. For example, eFax (*www.efax.com*) offers subscribers their own private fax number, which allows them to receive incoming faxes with their e-mail. (Free and fee-based options are available.) For a reasonable monthly fee, uReach (*www.ureach.com*) also offers Web faxing services, as well as toll-free phone numbers that track you down when you're out of the office, voicemail options, and other handy communications tools for the busy VA.

Checking Your Client's E-Mail From a Remote Computer

Once clients get to know their VAs, they often ask them to handle the more sensitive tasks, such as monitoring their e-mail for time-critical messages. Thankfully, checking your client's e-mail from your own computer is simple. With their user name and password, you can access their messages either through their e-mail provider's interface or via an independent Web-based e-mail application such as mail2web (*www.mail2web.com*). With these applications, you can manage your clients' e-mail as easily as you would your own.

Online Meetings and Collaboration

The Internet now enables VAs to work online in real time with their clients, shrinking the perceived distance between the two camps even further. Depending upon your niche, you may soon need such tools in your own practice and find that your clients are already using them.

A good example is Microsoft's NetMeeting, a real-time collaboration and conferencing application for virtual teams. NetMeeting is already installed on systems with a Windows 2000 operating system (to find it click "Start," "Programs," "Accessories," "Communications," and then "NetMeeting"). It can also be downloaded for free (*www.microsoft.com/windows/NetMeeting*). Using NetMeeting, a VA and her client can have "face-to-face" conversations with the audio and video conferencing features, participate in text-based chats, transfer files, share programs, and even create and share graphics on a virtual whiteboard. The various features are easy to master, but again you'll want to practice a bit with a friend or family member before going live with clients.

If the free tools don't fit the bill, you can also find fee-based options. Among the more popular are GoToMeeting (*www.gotomeeting.com*), WebEx (*www.webex.com*), and Live Meeting (*www.microsoft.com/office/livemeeting*).

Remote Desktop Sharing

Not long ago, we were speaking with a VA who told us that she routinely creates customized mailings, then prints them out immediately on her printer for distribution. On the surface, this sounds routine. But we've left out an important detail: She creates the mailings on her *client's* computer, more than 500 miles away.

As many VAs are, she's using GoToMyPC, a web-based "screen sharing" application that enables remote, secure access to other computers. The current favorite of the remote access world, GoToMyPC (*www.gotomypc.com*) unlocks many remote-work options without sacrificing security. The VA can troubleshoot a client's PC, or train a client in software use, from miles away. Similarly, if the client uses specialized software, the VA can run it as though she were sitting at the client's keyboard.

Of course, remote working relationships of this kind require a high level of trust. But the arrangement can be tailored with such options as "supervised control," which allows the VA access to some files or programs but not others. (Microsoft's free NetMeeting, previously discussed, which also includes a remote desktop-sharing feature, gives the client less leeway over access and security than does GoToMyPC. But for those on a tight budget, this option is worth checking into.)

Typically, the client will pay any fee associated with these applications (usually $20–30 per month), though some VAs with multiple client-users will pay for everyone's access, then factor it into their fees. Review vendors' sites carefully, so you fully understand an application's capabilities and features (pay particular attention to security) and have the client do the same. Be sure everyone is comfortable with the application and working arrangement before committing. If the vendor offers a trial period, take it and "kick the tires" before buying.

Relationship Maintenance

Despite all the marvelous collaboration tools available today, it's important to remember that even remote relationships are still more about people than technology. Even when the tech side is running as smoothly as a Swiss clock, make a point of communicating regularly with your clients by phone. Set up weekly "pulse check" calls if necessary, and use these occasions to make sure you and the client are focused on the same goals, so you don't inadvertently diverge or work at cross-purposes. If a client hasn't been giving you regular feedback, ask if he's satisfied with your performance and if there's anything else he'd like you to be working on. An occasional 10-minute phone call can be just the thing to remind both of you that there's a "real person" on each side of the virtual partnership.

Pointers, Tips, and a Few Pearls of Wisdom

In this section we're going to pull up a cracker barrel, fill coffee mugs all around, hook our false beards over our ears, and give you some final tips, pointers we've gathered from VAs around the world, and a few "pearls of wisdom." We've divided it into four categories: your business, clients, family, and taking care of the VA (you).

Take the ones that work best for you and post them in prominent places around your office or home. These "experienced sailors" will help you keep your ship on course.

Your Business

Co-author Chris's Vermonter grandfather used to tell her, "Miss Chris, if you're not careful, you're going to end up where you're going."

Success in business, as in life, requires a plan, a positive attitude, and an open mind. Lacking any of these, a VA will almost certainly end up where he or she is "going" instead of the destination he or she had hoped for.

Following are some pointers to consider as you move toward your intended business destination:

✿ Plan your work and work your plan. (And don't be afraid to change the plan.)

✿ Run your business; don't let it run you.

✿ A VA's worst enemies are disorganization, stale thinking, sloppy work habits, and mismanaged time and priorities.

✿ Don't mistake efficiency for effectiveness.

✦ Effectiveness means taking the shortest possible path to the right goals.

✦ Efficiency merely refers to accomplishing a given act with the minimum effort.

✦ Successful VAs serve their clients effectively and complete their tasks efficiently.

✿ Streamline your decision-making.

✦ A busy VA will make many stressful decisions each week.

✦ Making decisions quickly, rather than agonizing over them, helps reduce stress.

✦ Decisions with an emotional punch will always be tough. Don't fight it.

✦ Work to make the *process* simpler: Define the issue, identify the alternatives, gather data for each, consider implications, consult your gut, act.

✦ Don't second-guess yourself. Calculate, act, and move on.

★ Set reasonable goals. Don't demoralize yourself with unnecessary disappointments.

★ Don't give in to "urgency."

✦ When you start work each day, create a list of the most important tasks to be completed that day.

✦ Set aside your most productive time of day (for many, this is the morning) to work on those projects.

✦ Check e-mail every half hour on the half hour (or at other pre-set intervals) rather than every time a new message arrives.

✦ If you're in the middle of a pressing project, let voice mail get the phone. Interruptions will not only distract and delay you, but fatigue you as well.

✦ Break large projects down into smaller parts, and complete these regularly as you work toward your deadline. This will minimize those eleventh-hour "freak outs" that drain our health and disrupt our family life.

★ Work as though you're self-employed—you are!

★ Embrace change, even though the dose may sometimes be larger than you'd like. Change is an opportunity for growth.

★ Successful VAs are accountable VAs; don't blame others for errors and problems. (Businesspeople respect account-ability. So do children in parents.)

✸ Don't burn your bridges—let diplomacy be your theme. "Everyone knows someone," and "someone" may well be your next client.

✸ Don't work to exhaustion before taking time off. (Would *you* hire someone who looks the way that hollow-eyed VA in the mirror does?)

✸ Avoid or overcome procrastination.

◆ Prioritize your tasks, and manage them by number (not desire).

◆ Take a "focus hour" each day—voice mail on, e-mail alerts off—to concentrate on the day's top-priority project. This will assure timely progress.

◆ Take "mini-breaks" throughout the day, for a snack, short walk, deep-breathing exercises. These gaps will clear and reinvigorate your mind.

◆ Set deadlines that are slightly ahead of actual deadlines. This lets you add "post-deadline" polish and deliver impressive results (rather than merely adequate output).

Your Clients

We all know that "superior customer service" is the key to client loyalty and new business, but what does that mean? Every VA has her own unique philosophy, but a good rule of thumb might be this: Meet the client's needs on every level and then give them a little bit more.

Following are some tips on tending to your clients:

✸ Deliver your services in a memorable way.

◆ Keep a positive attitude.

◆ "Under-promise and over-deliver."

- ✦ Similarly, manage client expectations. ("No, we're not going to Disney World next week.")
- ✦ Whenever possible, deliver projects well *before* deadlines.
- ✦ Take pride in your business, yourself, your work.
- ✦ Get to know your clients and their personal details—and keep these handy for reference in communications—but don't try to your clients' "best friend."
- ✦ Treat your clients as partners rather than individuals.
- ✯ Avoid getting "too close to your clients." Working partnerships that become friendships are much harder to manage and can result in many hours of non-billable "small talk" and expectations of preferential treatment.
- ✯ Make your clients feel "comfortable."
  - ✦ Design your Website to say "welcome." Remember the three F's: fast, facts, and friendly.
  - ✦ Be genuine in your communications. (Use your language and tone rather than sterile business language.)
  - ✦ Smile when you speak on the phone.

Your Family

Rewarding though they may be, your days as a VA may sometimes seem to be a real balancing act, as you shoulder the needs of clients, family, business, and, with a stolen moment here and there, yourself. And ironically, the people you've built your world around and whose needs you're often striving foremost to meet—your family—can be the most challenging ball to juggle. Here are some thoughts on how to stay on the tightrope with everything in hand.

✹ Regulate your workflow according to your family's needs. (Don't bite off more than your family can chew.)

✹ Don't expect your family to make unlimited sacrifices as you plow ahead. It's not fair to them, and it will only hasten the uncomfortable days of reckoning.

✹ As with clients, manage your family's expectations. ("I told you. We're not going to Disneyworld next week.")

✹ Raising children and business under the same roof is much less stressful if you plan ahead:

  ✦ Establish a work routine that fits your children's schedule. It may be difficult at first, but children (especially younger ones) will quickly accept your working as just another part of their routine.

  ✦ Schedule high-focus tasks to coincide with your child's sleep or quiet play times.

  ✦ Try to keep the same hours each day, and schedule "kids only" time, too. Try combining a "hug break" with your coffee break.

✹ Take advantage of technology when the children are "a little out of control."

  ✦ If the house has gotten too noisy for business calls, let the voice mail pick up.

  ✦ Use the "mute" and "hold" buttons when little ones don't want to be mute or want to be held.

✹ Let your children see you working. (If they think your activities are a secret, they'll only clamor more to "uncover" them.)

✯ If you have the space, set up a small desk for your child next to your own, so you can "work together." Fill the drawers with crayons, colorful paper, coloring books, paste, and other items that will keep the child occupied while you work.

✯ Set up "visuals" to help children understand when you're not to be interrupted. For example, a red scarf on the doorknob can mean "Mom's on an important phone call."

2-Second Spotlight

Involving Children in Your Business
Name: Evy Williams

"My children help me fold flyers, stuff envelopes, and apply stamps. We sit around and talk while doing these chores so it's more enjoyable for everyone. My oldest daughter, a senior in high school, acts as my proofreader and editor for my written work. My middle daughter, a sophomore, wants to help me in my business to make money while attending college. I told her to learn how I do things and she can be a 'partner' when the time comes."

• • • • •

✯ Tell your children what type of behavior you expect when you're working. This will help reduce stress and flare-ups.

✯ Before you make or take a phone call, make an announcement: "I will be on the phone for a few minutes. No interruptions or loud noise please!"

✯ Reward your children for being good "partners" in your business. A batch of cookies, a movie, or a small toy from the prize jar to say "thank you for being so good" can help promote on-going cooperation.

✯ Place a box of quiet, "office only" toys in your work area. Tell your child that as long as he or she is quiet, they can play with these special toys right next to you.

✯ Ask your children how *you* are doing:

✦ "Am I spending enough time with you?"

✦ "What do you wish could be different?"

✦ "What do you like about me working at home?"

The VA (You)

In the midst of being "all things to all people," and plowing on toward business success, VAs often neglect their own physical and emotional needs. But *you* are the most important asset your business has. Without you, it's nothing more than a room with machines and paper inside. Take care of yourself and, just as importantly, be kind to yourself.

✯ Building a business is a marathon, not a sprint. If you're unhappy with a project of some other aspect of your business on any given day, don't let it throw you off track. Praise yourself for what went well, and move on.

✯ When you do something you're proud of, take a moment to write down how you did it and how it felt. This will help you see the business journey as a series of mini successes rather than one big lunge for a far-off goal.

✯ If you're feeling alone, consider partnering with another VA to exchange goals. Check in weekly to see how your "partner" is progressing.

✯ Avoid negative thinking and a darkened outlook:

✦ Surround yourself with strong people and avoid chronic complainers.

✦ Remember that the world is better than the headlines would have you believe.

✦ Don't go out of your way to spread bad news.

✦ Exercise often and eat well. Your feelings and your health are inseparable.

✦ Get plenty of rest. Fatigue can be demoralizing.

✦ Assert yourself. People who "stand up for themselves" are on the road to greater strength.

✦ Don't be afraid to quit. You may be pursuing the wrong path.

✦ Don't nurse grudges. (Among other things, they get in the way of business.) Let go and move on.

☆ Inspire yourself!

✦ Set the tone for your own day. You're the tuning fork for the song of your life.

✦ Bounce back quickly! If a client rejects a proposal or pitch, it's not the end of the world. Tap your tuning fork again and keep singing. "Yes" will come.

✦ Never take more time to tally your troubles than you do to count your blessings. Tallying troubles is a trouble in itself!

• • • • •

Here endeth our "Poor Richard's Almanac." Taken together, it represents a standard that no businessperson in her sane mind could expect to meet (just as Ben Franklin, the author of the original *Poor Richard*, occasionally fell short of his own). It's intended to let you "take what you need and leave the rest," and above all to help you keep that gleaming tuning fork tuned.

CHAPTER 10

The VA Toolbox: Resources and Information

During the American gold rush, whole towns had a way of popping up almost overnight. Gold miners and panners would flock to new areas intent on striking it rich, and close behind came the entrepreneurial merchants who knew the prospectors would need clothes, tools, food, and other saleable items. In no time, stores lined the streets and merchandise filled the stores. Boom towns were born.

In many ways, the Virtual Assistance industry is in its "boom town" phase and, as you'll see, there are "merchants" setting up shop along the virtual streets to meet the needs of those who are moving there. Regardless of what they're selling, these merchants have one thing in common: you. You are their target market. And it's up to you to decide who you'll do business with.

This chapter is a compilation of information about groups, organizations, certifications, and other resources for VAs. Besides general information, we've included special resource sections for work-at-home parents, VAs with disabilities, military and other "trailing" spouses, and even one for "cheapskates."

(To acknowledge the lawyers tugging at our coat sleeves, please note that the inclusion of a resource doesn't necessarily imply our endorsement, nor does its exclusion imply a thumbs-down.)

Virtual Assistant Trade Groups

Before we introduce you to some of the industry organizations for VAs, we'd be remiss if we didn't disclose our connection with some of the groups included in our list here. We own and manage Staffcentrix (*www.staffcentrix.com*) and MSVAs.com and founded the nonprofit International Virtual Assistants Association, commonly known as IVAA, in 1999. (For those who have an interest in the history of the VA industry, the story is at *www.ivaa.org/history-of-ivaa.htm.*) Shortly afterward, we turned IVAA over to its members, as planned at its founding, and have played no role in the organization since.

Research Before Joining

We suggest that you take the time to research a number of VA organizations before joining one or several, as your budget permits. These online professional organizations are a primary means of peer networking and can offer you important marketing venues, too, not to mention moral support, operational and growth tips, and more. Look for groups that have a high level of integrity and professionalism and that promote education and open dialogue among their members. As you compare your options, we suggest the following:

1. Contact the management of each organization, and ask them about their group and why you should consider joining them. Then evaluate:
    ✦ Did they reply promptly and answer your questions completely?

+ Do they show a solid understanding of the industry?

+ Is the tone of the reply friendly? Professional? Inviting?

+ Did they gratuitously "badmouth" other VA organizations?

+ Was the sales pitch too hard? Too soft? About right?

2. Contact a few random members of the organization.

+ Do they feel they're getting good value for their membership fee?

+ Would they recommend the group?

+ Do they feel a sense of community with fellow members?

+ What do they like best, and least, about the group?

3. Evaluate their Website.

+ Does the site contain information for prospective clients as well as for VAs?

+ Is it clear and easy to navigate?

+ Does it provide opportunities for exposure to your prospective clients (for example, listings in a directory, a request for proposal (RFP) service, media exposure)?

+ Is there an "about us" or "history" link that tells you who is at the helm and the background of the organization?

+ Is the leadership self-promotional or member-focused? Do links on the site seem to lead back too often to products and services being offered by the people who run the group?

4. Assessing the value: getting the biggest "bang for your buck."

  ✦ Membership fees can vary dramatically. Are they proportional to benefits?

  ✦ Are the marketing efforts of the organization strong? Global? Regional? Local?

  ✦ What venues are provided for interacting with fellow VAs (e-mail list, newsletter, bulletin board, and so forth)?

  ✦ Are the online resources for members extensive? Adequate? Thin?

  ✦ Do resources appear to be updated regularly?

A List of International VA Organizations, Associations, and Groups

A Clayton's Secretary	*www.asecretary.com.au*
A Virtual Solution	*www.avirtualsolution.com*
Alliance of UK Virtual Assistants	*www.allianceofukvirtual assistants.org.uk*
Association of Virtual Assistants of Ireland	*www.avaireland.com*
The Canadian Virtual Assistants Network	*www.canadianva.net*
International Association of Virtual Assistants	*www.iava.org.uk*
International Association of Virtual Office Assistants	*www.iavoa.com*
International Virtual Assistants Association	*www.ivaa.org*
MSVAS.com (Military Spouse VAs)	*www.msvas.com*
REVA Network (Real Estate Virtual Assistants)	*www.revanetwork.com*
Staffcentrix	*www.staffcentrix.com*
Work-the-Web.com	*www.work-the-web.com*

● ● ● ● ●

Independent E-Mail Lists and Networking Forums for VAs

In addition to the larger industry organizations just listed, which usually offer networking among other benefits or resources, independent or stand-alone networking groups have been developing as well. Because most VAs work alone or with their children, it's important that they feel connected to a larger whole—a bigger "family," if you will—and these groups can help. And they not only provide essential adult and professional contact, but they encourage a flow of fresh information, both of which stimulate growth in any startup business.

The majority of these groups are hosted by services such as CoolList (*www.coollist.com*), MSN Groups (*groups.msn.com*), and Yahoo! Groups (*groups.yahoo.com*). To explore your options and find the lists you like, simply visit these e-mail hosting sites and enter *"virtual assistant"* in their search feature. You'll find large groups and small, some open to the public and others for approved members only, and even those with a regional focus.

VA Certifications and Training

The growth of the Virtual Assistance industry has also led to an increasing number of VA-specific certifications, courses, and training programs, offered by larger VA organizations and community colleges or by groups of individual VAs who have formed specialized certification companies. Their rapid rise has sparked debate among VAs as to how these should all be valued and which, if any, they should pursue.

In our own experience, we have seen many VAs launch and grow their businesses with little or no training, though many others have opted for VA-specific preparation before going on to succeed. (We ourselves, as we've mentioned periodically in earlier chapters, offer VA training programs, as we have for years.)

The main issues for the aspiring VA, it seems to us, are *need* and *resources,* and these vary greatly from individual to individual. For example, if your niche-specific skill sets—in bookkeeping, or executive assistance, or graphic design, and so on—are strong, and your budget is limited, and you have some entrepreneurship experience and a good feel for the Internet, then maybe you should simply go straight to the marketplace. On the other hand, if your niche skill sets are weak, and you have little or no business experience, but you have the budget, you might consider a two-pronged approach: polishing your niche credentials with skill-specific training and signing up concurrently for an in-depth VA training program. In another permutation (as you can imagine, there are many), if your skill sets are weak but your home-based business background is strong, then your money might be better spent on niche-specific training only.

In terms of cost, VA training programs in general range from online clusters priced at a few hundred dollars to comprehensive community college certificate and credit programs (offered increasingly now in the United States, and also in Canada) priced commensurately higher. We have not "field-tested" any of these programs ourselves, but for reference you can find a community college-level VA certificate program described at the Website of California's MiraCosta College (*www.miracosta.edu/home/kstriebel/virtual_assistant.htm*) or at the site of Alberta, Canada's Red Deer College (*www.rdc.ab.ca/ office_administration/va_certificate.html*). Among programs offered exclusively online (though it may not fit everyone's budget) we have heard good things about Stacy Brice's training at AssistU (*www.assistu.com*).

Niche-Specific Certifications

Whether you've been out of the workforce for a while or steadily employed all your life, you may want to upgrade the skills that you're planning to sell to your target market. Often, niche-specific certifications are the first thing your prospects will want to see and, in the high-paced and ever-competitive services marketplace, which thanks to the Internet is now global, credentials can quickly lose their luster or go out of date.

In addition to training at their local community college or tech school, VAs seeking to improve their credentials inexpensively and quickly might well consider using BrainBench (*www.brainbench.com*), an online testing and certification company that has gained widespread respect among hirers. Brainbench offers more than 600 tests, ranging from the basic (typing speed and accuracy), to the specialized (financial industry knowledge), to the esoteric (Unix Korn Shell scripting).

Resources and Information for Homeschooling VAs

Unfortunately, our contemporary economy and lifestyle have forced many people to move to sprawling, gridlocked suburbs, where family life, roots, and long-standing values are all put at risk. But despite the transient sprawl context, many homeschooling families are leading the way to reclaiming small-town values and rediscovering the joy and strength of family bonds.

Yet as wonderful as homeschooling may be, the bills for day-to-day living expenses continue to come in the mailbox, and the need to set aside funds for college, vacation, retirement, and unforeseen emergencies, with one parent staying at home, can put considerable strain on the family budget. Ironically, however, it is technology—the very thing that has pulled so many people into the rat race—that now enables many homeschooling parents to work from home and balance career, family, *and* the budget.

2-Second Spotlight

Interview with Homeschool.com Co-Founder

Name:	Rebecca Kochenderfer, Senior Editor & Co-Founder
Business:	Homeschool.com, Inc.
URL:	*www.homeschool.com*
Personal:	Rebecca Kochenderfer is co-founder and senior editor of Homeschool.com, co-author of *Homeschooling for Success: How Parents Can Create A Superior Education For Their Child,* and a homeschooling mother of three.

A respected authority in the homeschooling arena, Rebecca's site draws more than 2 million visitors each year and has been selected by *Forbes* Magazine as the #1 homeschooling site on the Internet.

Q: *How can home-based self-employment benefit parents who are homeschooling or would like to?*

A: Homeschooling is a lot easier if you can work from your home because you have so much more flexibility and you do not lose time commuting back and forth. The children also benefit by seeing and perhaps even helping you with your work. Working from home makes it a lot easier to get the money you need while still homeschooling your children.

Q: *What are some of the benefits for children who see self-employed parents working in the home?*

A: My own children are very involved with Homeschool.com. They have had a chance to be interviewed on the radio, they have met famous scientists, they test and review educational products, and we all work together to assemble our homeschooling kits. Even their friends like to help! They like to know that someone is listening to their ideas and that we care about their opinions. Most importantly, I hope that I have set a good example for them by doing work that I love and that has such meaning for me. Hopefully they will also be able to find fulfilling, meaningful work when they grow up.

• • • • •

Homeschooling VAs have often told us of the wealth of lessons that children can learn, directly and indirectly, from the business, particularly when they see Mom or Dad acting in a professional capacity. The lessons learned may fall into the "three R's" or involve much deeper questions—even profound questions—of the value of self-reliance and honor, and service to others.

For example, on the academic level, a younger child who helps even with a simple filing task will enhance his alphabetization skills, and an older child who helps with invoicing or accounting can learn a great deal about the practical application of math. More fundamentally, children who are involved in the business even passively, as observers (as all children are so acutely)—as they watch Mom or Dad honor commitments, negotiate with clients, or simply produce and distribute work—can learn invaluable lessons about ethics, responsibility, teamwork, when to compromise and when to push back, and the justified pride of a job well done.

Homeschooling Resources on the Internet

Homeschool.com	*www.homeschool.com*
The Home School Mom	*www.thehomeschoolmom.com*
Teaching Kids Business:	*www.teachingkidsbusiness.com*
HomeschoolBuzz.com	*www.homeschoolbuzz.com*
Homeschoolers' Curriculum Swap	*www.theswap.com*
Time4Learning	*www.time4learning.com*

• • • • •

Resources and Information for Military and Other "Trailing" Spouses

"Trailing spouses" (we prefer the term "accompanying partners") are women and men who give up their jobs or other priorities to follow their spouse in an employment-related move to a new location. Those married to people in the military, the Foreign Service, multinational corporations, or a variety of government agencies often find themselves "trailing." And although the lifestyle can offer some wonderful perks, it can also wreak havoc with the accompanying partner's career (not to mention morale and self-esteem).

These frequent moves leave spouses with resumes that, from an employer's perspective, shout *"job-hopper!"* from beginning to end. Compounding the problem are relocations that can take spouses to isolated posts, high cost-of-living areas, or, in the case of international moves, countries that impose strict regulations on the employment of non-citizens.

Now, however, the "portability" of a VA practice allows the spouse to build a business that travels with the family and can continue to grow and thrive almost regardless of location. (A few countries, however, through treaties or other laws, may restrict almost *all* types of economic activity by the non-citizen. Check with your appropriate legal advisor or other authority for details.) The end result is a relationship in which there is no longer a "leader" and a "trailer," but rather two equal partners—as it should be.

Trade Your Wrecked Resume for a Powerful Bio

As a Virtual Assistant, you are the owner and CEO/president/director of your own business rather than an employee, and this distinction lets you finally leave that "choppy" resume behind. Though resumes are at the core of traditional hiring, VAs usually prefer—altogether appropriately—to present their work history, accomplishments, and skills in the form of a "professional bio." This format conveys all that your prospective clients need to know about you, while eliminating the minute chronology of your prior employment—those pesky "from" and "to" dates associated with each job you've held.

You'll find thousands of examples of professional bios on the Net and VA-specific bios on your colleagues' Websites. But if you're in a hurry, *The Wall Street Journal* published some years ago an excellent article on bios, which can be found at *www.careerjournal.com/jobhunting/resumes/19981029-richardson.html.*

Military Spouses

The mobility requirements of a modern military (usually moving families every two to three years) can place severe burdens on the career and employment prospects of the service member's spouse. Employers hesitate to hire people who will likely have to pull up stakes within 36 months, so military spouses, in spite of their qualifications, are often passed over in favor of employees with stronger ties to the community. Adding insult to injury, every time a military family moves and a spouse has to leave her job (presuming she's been able to find one), she loses seniority and everything that comes with it. Thankfully, the VA career option has already made a substantial difference in the lives of many of these women and men who have been unfairly disadvantaged for so long.

Base Housing and the VA Practice

To date, we know of no VA who has been prohibited from launching a VA practice in base housing. However, where military regulations are concerned (not news to military spouses), it always pays to be on the safe side, so be sure to request permission from the housing office before starting your business. Typically, they'll want to know that the business will not generate additional vehicular traffic, involve hazardous materials or other extended inventory, or include signage indicating the presence of a business. In other words, they want to avoid businesses that create an "industrial presence" in a residential neighborhood.

2-Second Spotlight

VAing and the Military Lifestyle
Name: Mary Hern

There's something amazing about being part of the military community. You never know what to expect from each new location. Sometimes it involves a new social structure or a much different climate. Some neighborhoods are full of life and social interaction and some are inhabited by proverbial wallflowers that rarely venture out of doors. For the spouse of an active duty member, this type of hermit-filled community can make the experience trying to say the least. With no continuity in co-workers or friends and usually a residence that's a good distance from close family, the quality of life can suffer. This is where being a VA has been more than a financial benefit...it's been a lifeline.

Recently my husband and I lived in a location of closed doors and quiet neighbors. Interaction with the families on our street was non-existent. While stationed there, I found that my clients and those in my VA network really helped make me feel less isolated. Having a familiar social circle (albeit virtual) helped to keep me connected with others who had interests and ideals much like my own. For a social creature like myself, that's priceless.

...and 2 Seconds More on the "Portability" of a VA Practice

Several weeks ago my husband, our three children (two kids/one dog), and I embarked on a Permanent Change of Station to Langley AFB, VA. It took one week to travel to our base (stop at Grandma's), one week to be assigned a house (Temporary Living Facility), and another week to have our belongings delivered and moved in. When my husband arrived at his new office, it took him a full workweek to meet everyone in the office and figure out what they do. His training will continue for several more weeks and then he can begin the process of becoming an asset to the team. Phew! That's a long transition.

However, I was officially offline for four days during all this and had no breaks in the continuity or quality of work for my clients, and I was able to bring old coworkers and friends along with me to my new home more than a thousand miles away. It doesn't get any better than this. What other career offers such great benefits along with rewarding work?

• • • • •

Military Spouse Resources on the Internet

A comprehensive list of online resources for military spouses would require a book in itself, but here is a sampling of sites that carry work- or business-related information for spouses, many of which will link to other sites of equal use or interest.

Military Spouse Entrepreneurship	*www.onlinewbc.gov/ militaryspouses.html*
Military Spouses Career Network	*www.mscn.org*
Open Directory List of Links	*dmoz.org/Society/Military/ People/Spouses*
National Military Family Association	*www.nmfa.org*
LIFELines Services Network	*www.lifelines2000.org*
Military Assistance Program (DoD)	*www.dod.mil/mapsite*
Air Force Crossroads	*www.afcrossroads.com*

Army Community Service	*www.armycommunityservice.org*
Sgt. Mom's Place	*www.sgtmoms.com*
4MilitaryFamilies.com	*www.4militaryfamilies.com*
Military Living Publications	*www.militaryliving.com*
Shore Duty (Sarah Smiley)	*www.sarahsmiley.com*
MilSpouse.org	*www.milspouse.org*
CinCHouse	*www.cinchouse.com*

● ● ● ● ●

Foreign Service Spouses

Co-author Michael Haaren was a Foreign Service dependent in 1966–1967, when he lived in Thailand with his Uncle Ben (a career USIA officer) and Aunt Betty Anne. As a teenager caught up in the excitement of Bangkok, he had little appreciation of the adjustments his aunt was making daily in living the Foreign Service life. She was always gracious and supportive in her role (though she would sometimes argue at the astonishing traffic) and even somehow helped him get his grade point average up at the International School Bangkok. Since then, however, he has come to realize the many personal sacrifices she had to have made to enable her husband to pursue his career.

Life as a Foreign Service (FS) spouse can involve moving self and family to a new country—some much further afield than Bangkok—every few years. The majority of FS spouses we've spoken with are pragmatic and optimistic people who see the lifestyle as offering unique experiences and opportunities. But even the most upbeat among them often find the impact on their careers difficult.

2-Second Spotlight

The Importance of "Portability" for Spouses on the Move

Name: Jan Fischer Bachman, President

Company: Creative Arts Consultancy

URL: *www.creativeartsconsultancy.com*

Personal: Jan has lived and worked in the UK, China, Mexico, the Dominican Republic, the Bahamas, and the United States. A Foreign Service spouse for more than a decade, she now runs a company that specializes in providing innovative services and products, including personal and business coaching, training programs incorporating hands-on arts activities, and creative marketing materials and publications.

Maintaining a career while making multiple international moves can be extremely challenging for Foreign Service spouses, because expertise in one country does not necessarily equal employment in the next. Many embassy jobs come with minimal responsibility and pay—$8 an hour is not uncommon—whereas employment on the local economy could mean legal complications or undesirable salaries. Even in countries with work agreements and reasonable pay, it can take months to build up a network leading to quality employment— just in time to move again!

Foreign Service support systems promote the idea of "portable careers," a concept aided by technological advances. Virtual gatherings can replace face-to-face meetings. E-mail groups facilitate worldwide professional networking, and the price of making an international call has dropped tremendously in many locations.

Internet printing (*www.kinkos.com*, for example) allows products to be delivered from anywhere within hours.

Difficulties remain, however. Internet access in some countries is slow, censored, sporadic, or very expensive. Adequate postal facilities do not exist everywhere (and restrictions on business usage apply to provisions such as the diplomatic pouch or armed forces postal services). Laws about international telecommuting can be unclear. Moving itself is time-consuming and disruptive. (It's pretty hard to meet deadlines while your computer sits in a box somewhere and the local ISP tells you that they will have your service up and running "soon.") Finally, capturing new U.S. clients can be daunting when you live in a different country. Even with the growth of electronic marketplaces, assignments commonly come through personal contacts or referrals. Networking from afar can be a challenging task, and some clients still prefer at least one initial face-to-face meeting.

The need for structural and legislative change still exists, and assistance in locating new clients would be extremely helpful, but virtual employment still offers the brightest possibilities for Foreign Service spouses and partners today.

• • • • •

Foreign Service Spouse Resources on the Internet

Associates of the American Foreign Service Worldwide	*www.aafsw.org*
Dept. of State (Family Liaison Office)	*www.state.gov/m/dghr/flo*
American Foreign Service Association	*www.afsa.org*
Foreign Service Youth Foundation	*www.fsyf.org*
Foreign Service Community Assoc. (Canada)	*www.fsca-acse.org*
ExpatExchange	*www.expatexchange.com*

• • • • •

Resources and Information for Work-at-Home Parents

Despite running a large company with international interests, we are both predominantly work-at-home parents: Chris's children are both at home, and Mike's youngest is often flitting about as he works. So we know firsthand the issues (and crises) that have to be juggled when work and family mix. Because we've already covered the topic of raising children and a business under the same roof, we'll just pass along briefly a few of the many work-at-home-parent Websites we've found useful over the years.

Internet Resources for Moms

Home-Based Working Moms	*www.hbwm.com*
Moms@Home Working	*www.moms-home-work.com*
WorkOptions.com	*www.workoptions.com*
Work At Home Mom (WAHM)	*www.wahm.com*
Generation Mom	*www.generationmom.com*
WAHMFest	*www.wahmfest.org*
The Entrepreneurial Parent	*www.en-parent.com*

• • • • •

Internet Resources for Dads

The Fatherhood Project	*www.fatherhoodproject.org*
National Center for Fathering	*www.fathers.com*
Slowlane.com	*www.slowlane.com*
Work-at-Home Dad Central	*www.en-parent.com/ EPcenters/WAHD-Central.htm*
The Entrepreneurial Parent	*www.en-parent.com*

• • • • •

Resources and Information for VAs With Disabilities

In working with thousands of entrepreneurs internationally, we've discovered that many people with disabilities, in business or out, embody an exceptional entrepreneurial aptitude and fire—traits that can only come from a life filled with challenges. Whether a person is born with a disability or develops an impairment later in life, he or she faces barriers that most people would be hard-pressed to imagine.

The Virtual Assistant option has brought significant opportunity to many people with disabilities already, particularly to those dealing with challenging mobility issues. No longer do transportation and access barriers have to prevent an individual from pursuing a career or receiving fair remuneration for his or her professional skills. Though not a panacea, the development of virtual careers and employment signals a major shift in the career and employment outlook for people with disabilities who want or need to work from home.

Accessible Technology

Though there is much to be done, developers of assistive technology (AT) are moving ahead on many fronts. For an update, we spoke briefly with Microsoft Accessibility Technology Group Product Manager Gary Moulton, a long-standing champion of accessible technology and co-author of the book *Accessible Technology in Today's Business* (Microsoft Press, 2002). Gary alerted us to a study by Forrester Research commissioned by Microsoft in 2003, which found that an impressive 57 percent of computer users are "likely or very likely" to benefit from accessible technology, with 44 percent already using it.

Gary also pointed out that there is "an AT product now for almost every kind of disability" and noted that the compatibility issues often arising in AT development are being addressed in part through Microsoft's Assistive Technology Vendor Program (MATvp). The MATvp, which works with software and hardware developers internationally, includes such innovative companies as Switzerland-based QualiLife, SA. Gary noted that QualiLife was recently chosen to provide comprehensive accessibility software solutions to patients at the SUVA Rehabilitation Hospital in Sion, whose TV sets are being replaced with computers. (For further information on the MATvp, see *www.microsoft.com/enable/at/matvplist.aspx.*)

Internet Resources for VAs With Disabilities

Disabled Entrepreneurs Network	*www.disabled-entrepreneurs.net*
The Abilities Fund	*www.abilitiesfund.org*
Australian Entrepreneurs with Disabilities	*www.aeda.asn.au*
Intl. Ctr for Disability Resources on the Internet	*www.icdri.org*
Entrepreneurs with Disabilities Network	*www.e-d-n.net*
The Center for an Accessible Society	*www.accessiblesociety.org*
EnabledOnline.com	*www.enabledonline.com*
Diversity World	*www.diversityworld.com*
DisabilityInfo.gov	*www.disabilityinfo.gov*
Disabled Businesspersons Association	*www.disabledbusiness.com*
Microsoft Accessibility Technology	*www.microsoft.com/enable*

• • • • •

Resources and Information for the Frugal VA

If we haven't mentioned bootstrapping lately, don't worry, here it comes again. The frugal VA will always be our hero (next to ineffective marketing, the second-biggest threat to the VA practice is debt). Providentially, the Internet has plenty of great "freebies" for small business owners, some of which we'll share with you here.

IRS (Small Business Resource Guide, CD-ROM)

www.irs.gov/businesses/small/page/0,,id=7128,00.html

The "Small Business Resource Guide, CD-ROM" provides critical tax information for small businesses, including forms, instructions, and publications. The CD also includes valuable business information from a variety of government agencies, non-profit organizations, and educational institutions, with other essential startup information. Easy to use, and definitely worth a look.

The FreeSite.com (Various Freebies)

www.thefreesite.com

The "home of the Web's best freebies" has proven to be an invaluable resource for many new home-based "e-entrepreneurs." The owner of the site scours the Net looking for free offers of all kinds, and many of those listed are great for VAs on a tight budget. Goodies include online calendars, encryption software, Webmaster tools, graphics, and even a few freebies for the other members of your family.

VistaPrint (Free Business Cards)

www.vistaprint.com

We've heard from many VAs who were delighted with their orders of 250 free business cards from VistaPrint. The only fee is shipping and handling, which is usually less than $5 for orders shipped in the United States—a small price for quality business cards.

eFax (Receive Faxes Without a Fax Machine)

www.efax.com

As we mentioned earlier, if you aren't ready to buy a fax machine yet but want the ability to receive faxes from your clients, eFax could be the way to go. When you sign up for their free account option, you'll be assigned a fax number, and incoming faxes will be sent to you via e-mail. (A more robust fee-based service is also available.)

Mail2Web (Check E-Mail From Any Computer)

www.mail2web.com

This free online application, also worth mentioning again, enables you to check your e-mail (or your clients') from any computer. Simply type in the e-mail address and password and all messages on the server will display. Unless you delete a message, it will stay on the server for download at your regular workstation.

Press Release Distribution Services

When you write a press release and would like to distribute it beyond your local or regional media outlets, you'll probably want to use a PR distribution service. Typically, these services submit your press release to major search engines, newswires, and a variety of Websites, maximizing your audience. Services that offer free distribution will generally offer a paid option as well. In most cases the free service will do the trick, but you may want to spring for the paid service to reach a specific market more effectively.

Free-Press-Release.com	*www.free-press-release.com*
PR Leap	*www.prleap.com*
Click2NewSites.com	*www.click2newsites.com*
USANews Release Network	*www.usanews.net*
PR Web	*www.prweb.com*
Eworldwire Press Release Service	*www.prfree.com*

• • • • •

FreeConference.com (Free Conference Calls)

www.freeconference.com

Here, you can arrange scheduled or unscheduled conference calls for up to 100 people at no charge. Callers are billed by their regular long-distance provider (if the call is long distance for them) at their usual rate per minute. There is also a toll-free plan—eliminating long-distance tolls for the individual callers—which charges you 10 cents per minute per participant.

Document Conversion to PDF

PDF (portable document format) documents are popular because they retain their structure when moved from one system to another and are not easily manipulated the way *.doc* or *.rtf* files can be.

In the past, one had to purchase expensive Adobe software to create PDFs. Now, services such as PDFonline (*www.pdfonline.com*) are making document conversion free and easy. Simply upload your document, enter your e-mail address, and click send. In less than a minute (usually), your converted document will arrive as a PDF attachment in your e-mail.

Index

About the Authors

Christine Durst

Chris Durst is credited with having founded the Virtual Assistant industry in her home in rural Connecticut in 1995, with the launch of the Internet-based My Staff, LLC. In 1999, with Michael Haaren, she founded the International Virtual Assistants Association—the industry's nonprofit parent organization—and served as its first president.

As the co-founder and CEO of Staffcentrix, LLC, Chris spearheaded the development of groundbreaking virtual career training programs for such clients as the Department of the Army and the Department of State. She has appeared in numerous media outlets, including *Forbes, Business Week, Fortune,* the *Singapore Straits Times*, and the *London Times*, as well as radio and TV, and her presentations on virtual careers include several presidential committees and the United Nations. She resides in Woodstock, Connecticut, with her two children.

Michael Haaren

An ex–Wall Street attorney, Mike was raised in a log cabin in the Shenandoah Valley of Virginia, and, as does Chris, remains a firm believer in the values of small-town life. He is the co-founder and COO of Staffcentrix, LLC, and co-founder of the International Virtual Assistants Association, serving as its first vice president.

Mike is a recognized authority on virtual careers and is the editor-in-chief of "The Rat Race Rebellion," a widely-read weekly bulletin of screened telework and freelance jobs. His articles have appeared in such publications as *Military Spouse Magazine, Paraplegia News,* and the *American Foreign Service Association Journal,* and he is often quoted in the media, including *The Wall Street Journal, Fortune, Inc., Business Week,* and many others. The great-grandson of the 15th Commandant of the Marine Corps, Mike served in the Army from 1968 to 1970. He graduated Phi Beta Kappa from Georgetown University and received his Juris Doctor from the University of Virginia.